D1446470

Pattern Breakers

WHY SOME START-UPS CHANGE THE FUTURE

Mike Maples Jr. &
Peter Ziebelman

PUBLICAFFAIRS

New York

PublicAffairs
Hachette Book Group
1290 Avenue of the Americas, New York, NY 10104
www.publicaffairsbooks.com
@Public_Affairs

Printed in Canada
First Edition: July 2024

Published by PublicAffairs, an imprint of Hachette Book Group, Inc. The PublicAffairs name and logo is a registered trademark of the Hachette Book Group.

The Hachette Speakers Bureau provides a wide range of authors for speaking events. To find out more, go to hachettespeakersbureau.com or email HachetteSpeakers@hbgusa.com.

PublicAffairs books may be purchased in bulk for business, educational, or promotional use. For information, please contact your local bookseller or Hachette Book Group Special Markets Department at special.markets@hbgusa.com.

The publisher is not responsible for websites (or their content) that are not owned by the publisher.

Print book interior design by Sheryl Kober

Library of Congress Cataloging-in-Publication Data
Names: Maples, Mike, Jr., author. | Ziebelman, Peter, author.
Title: Pattern breakers : why some start-ups change the future / Mike Maples Jr., Peter Ziebelman.
Description: First edition. | New York : PublicAffairs, 2024. | Includes index.
Identifiers: LCCN 2023047012 | ISBN 9781541704350 (hardcover) | ISBN 9781541704374 (ebook)
Subjects: LCSH: New business enterprises. | Venture capital.
Classification: LCC HD62.5 .M3556 2024 | DDC 658.1/1—dc23/eng/20231010
LC record available at https://lccn.loc.gov/2023047012
ISBNs: 9781541704350 (hardcover); 9781541704374 (ebook)

MRQ

Printing 1, 2024

To Julie, my greatest co-conspirator in the adventures
that matter most.
—Mike

To Cindy, you keep my feet on the ground
as I reach beyond my grasp.
—Peter

CONTENTS

INTRODUCTION

What's Luck Got to Do with It?

Humans are expert pattern matchers.

Each day greets us with rituals and routines, in how we wake up, ready the kids for school, or wind down after a day's work. Beyond our everyday habits, we also adapt to the collective patterns of our communities, resulting in smoother social interactions and a sense of belonging.

In business, "best practices" codify what works best. Executives look for patterns in past data to forecast the future. Managers gauge potential new hires from their previous performance. Public companies must report their finances according to generally accepted accounting principles.

Pattern matching guides almost all human activity. Neuroscience suggests the reason why: our brains are designed for it, to help us find order, predictability, and safety in an otherwise chaotic world. Drawing from past experiences and knowledge, our minds can process new information more efficiently, streamlining decision making. This ability also helps us bond with others and find our place in the community. It also contributes to academic success, enhanced social reputation, and a longer, richer life.

And that's why so few of us create breakthroughs.

Breakthroughs require pattern *breaking*.

Pattern-breaking founders create something that breaks the mold. Their pattern-breaking ideas boldly challenge us to depart from current habits.

Many of us consider these pattern-breaking ideas impossible or unthinkable—at first. Ironically, the experts we respect most are often the least able to see the potential for a break from the past. Often it is the outsider, unburdened by the past, who becomes the pattern-breaking person behind a pattern-breaking idea.

Consider the breakthrough of human flight.

George Melville, the US Navy's chief engineer, called aviation a "useless dream" in 1901. Two years later, the *New York Times* published a piece, "Flying Machines Which Do Not Fly," that foresaw the accomplishment of human flight as something that might be conquered in the very distant future. Here's how the article ended: "The flying machine which will really fly might be evolved by the combined and continuous efforts of mathematicians and mechanicians in from one million to ten million years. . . . To the ordinary man it would seem as if effort might be employed more profitably."

Fortunately, the Wright brothers weren't ordinary. They flew their first plane at Kitty Hawk, North Carolina, sixty-nine days after that *Times* editorial.

Orville and Wilbur Wright were not formally trained in physics or aeronautics. They owned a bicycle sales and repair shop in Dayton, Ohio. But they exemplified the independent thinking and peculiar mix of life experiences that often lead to a breakthrough. The principles they understood about balancing and steering bicycles significantly contributed to their eventual understanding of flight control.

Despite the experts' staunch belief that human flight was a fantasy, the Wright brothers defied the odds and shattered age-old perceptions. What they lacked in credentials they more than made up for with curiosity, persistent tinkering, analytical observation, practical mechanical skills, and sheer determination.

George Bernard Shaw captured their spirit in his play *Man and Superman*:

> *The reasonable man adapts himself to the world: the unreasonable one persists in trying to adapt the world to himself. Therefore, all progress depends on the unreasonable man.*

Shaw grasped an essential truth: Those who thrive within the current rules ("reasonable" people) are not the ones who steer us to new horizons. Breakthrough progress comes from the "unreasonable"—those who won't fit the mold, who see a different world and bend it to their will—the Pattern Breakers.

My job is to back unreasonable people who have unreasonable ideas, long before the rest of the world believes in them. For the past two decades at the venture capital firm Floodgate, I've invested in pattern-breaking founders and their pattern-breaking start-ups at the very beginning of their journeys.

Today, Floodgate is known as a pioneer and leader in the niche world of seed investing. I cofounded Floodgate in 2005 and helped define seed investing as a new category in venture capital. Unlike traditional investing, seed investing often involves backing just a couple of founders with an idea or possibly an early prototype with virtually no customers or historical financial information.

Our venture team has been fortunate to be the first investors in and to work at the earliest stages with some of the most dynamic breakthrough start-ups of the last two decades: X/Twitter, Twitch, Okta, Lyft, Rappi, and many others that have become household names or critical to the operations of major corporations. (Sadly, I've passed on more than a few breakthrough companies too. I'll discuss that a bit later.)

As seed investors, we have a very specific risk profile. We typically lose all our money in most of our investments, pinning our hopes on the occasional massive payoff when a start-up is wildly successful.

Investing into a start-up isn't like investing on Wall Street, where you can buy or sell at any time. Once we invest in an early-stage company, we stick with it until it is acquired by a larger company or it goes public on a stock exchange. Each investment journey can take several years, and there's no off-ramp in the interim.

Due to these factors, seed investing is deeply personal to me. I often say I invest in people I'd gladly get into trouble with, because trouble happens just about every single time. I pride myself on being more than just a financier. I'm a co-conspirator with ambitious founders in their rebellions against the status quo.

The breakthrough start-ups we have backed were all led by pattern-breaking founders who challenged conventional wisdom and convinced others to embrace a radically different future. They achieved this through a combination of pattern-breaking *ideas* that were radically different and pattern-breaking *actions* that persuaded the rest of the world to think, feel, and act differently.

Pattern-breaking ideas offer something radically different from anything that's come before. At first, these ideas can seem crazy. Why would anyone stay in a stranger's home? Yet Airbnb proved they would. Why would someone catch a ride in a stranger's car? Uber and Lyft, having dispatched tens of billions of passenger rides, answered that question. How could 140-character "tweets" ignite the most explosive media revolution of the last two decades? X/Twitter, with its simplicity, transformed the media and the public square.

Despite the initial strangeness of these transformative companies, their very uniqueness gave them enormous strength. They eluded the comparison trap, for there was often no precedent to measure them against. Instead of besting their rivals, they stood alone.

Throughout this book, you'll see why better ideas aren't enough. Remarkably *different* ideas are essential for achieving a massive impact. While pattern-breaking founders envision a different future through their ideas, that's not all there is to it. They must pull others along with them to make their ideas real. Asking the world to leave the known for an unsure tomorrow is a provocative act. It's unsettling to most. So these founders don't win by blending into the crowd or following conventional approaches.

Instead, they persuade others to change their habits through their pattern-breaking actions. They draw a stark dichotomy between the world as it exists and the world as it could be, urging us to embark on a journey to a different future with them.

Because their ideas and actions are so radical, pattern breakers often face the fierce resistance of a world reluctant to change. Often their closest advisors and family try to bring them back into the mainstream, critics scorn them, incumbent corporations try to defeat them, and sometimes governments even try to outlaw them. But they forge ahead, driven by a purpose far beyond conventional acceptance.

JUST A LUCKY FOOL?

In August 2014, I was feeling particularly uneasy, and not because of an embarrassing investment failure. It was because of an unexpected investment windfall. I had backed the start-up that became Twitch from its beginnings seven years earlier. Since then, Twitch had attracted tens of millions of users. Then Amazon acquired it for close to $1 billion.

But the investment success felt like a forward fumble. The original idea I'd backed many years earlier was very different from the product Amazon had acquired: it was originally an internet reality show called Justin.tv that featured cofounder Justin Kan livestreaming his daily activities 24/7. After a few years and a lot of major course corrections, Justin.tv launched Twitch as a separate entity.

Twitch's popularity had skyrocketed, but I hadn't fully understood why.

I checked in with Spencer, my fourteen-year-old son and resident video game and YouTube expert. "What's the big deal about Twitch?" I asked.

He looked confused. "I thought you invested in Twitch?!"

Spencer gave me a quick tour of live channels from streamers with names like Captainsparklez, PhantomL0rd, and Nightblue3. Over a hundred thousand people were simultaneously watching someone play League of Legends—more spectators than you'd see in stadiums for major sporting events. Another streamer owned the world record for "speed runs" through Super Mario 64.

It blew my mind. These streamers weren't movie icons or rock stars, at least not how I understood it. They were ordinary people playing video games. Yet some had massive followings any celebrity would envy. Why would anyone—let alone millions of people—tune in to watch some random person play a video game? It challenged my beliefs about entertainment and fame.

But that wasn't all that unsettled me. That same week, a start-up founder I would have pegged for near-certain success shuttered his company. Again, I didn't fully understand why. He'd raised money from some of Silicon Valley's sharpest investors and had excelled at all the things he was supposed to—customer development, finding a big market, building a great team, and defining a high-performance culture. His start-up could've been a case study of what to do. Except it failed. After years of sacrifice, waves of layoffs, and waning morale, investors and supporters lost faith. He lived the agony of watching his start-up slowly die.

And this kind of event—a start-up that seemed to do the right things yet still failed—wasn't isolated. I saw it happen again and again.

I had calculated that more than 80 percent of the most impactful start-ups I'd worked with had pivoted. That is, they'd moved in a new direction that differed—often quite radically—from their starting point.

Twitter wasn't Twitter when I invested in 2005. It was a podcasting company called Odeo. But when Apple made podcasting free in iTunes, Odeo was in deep trouble. Twitter, called twttr at the time, was started by Jack Dorsey, Evan Williams, and Biz Stone as they frantically searched for a new direction.

I invested in Twitch when it was a live internet reality show called Justin.tv. Four years later, it transformed into the streaming platform we now recognize as Twitch.

Chegg was a classified site for colleges when we provided seed funding in 2006. When it went public in November 2013, it provided a range of educational services totally unrelated to its original service.

Lyft was called Zimride when we seed-funded it in 2010. It was originally designed for carpooling at colleges and companies. In 2012, it shifted its focus to become the ridesharing service we recognize today.

The founders of Zimride executed extremely well in their shift. But you might be surprised to learn that many founders of breakthrough start-ups didn't necessarily plan or execute better than the founders whose ventures never took off.

Take X/Twitter for example. The founders differed on the vision. They kept changing who was in charge. The "Fail Whale" frequently appeared due to site overload, which happened almost every day.

There was chaos during the early days of Twitch as well. Emmett Shear, the CEO, has been open about the management dysfunction back then, marked by unclear roles, cultural challenges, competing visions, and the struggle to make decisions at pivotal moments.

Since pattern-breaking start-ups often shifted their initial ideas, and great execution didn't always guarantee success, a deeper concern came to mind: maybe the success or failure of the start-ups I'd chosen was due to dumb luck.

The Lucky Fool is a key character in Nassim Taleb's *Fooled by Randomness* (one of my favorite books). The lucky fool succeeds mostly due to luck, but in hindsight he ascribes the success to something else—not to good fortune, but to skill or strategy or genius or work ethic or some other factor that he tailors to fit the facts.

Was I being fooled by randomness? Were the breakout founders I worked with lucky fools? Was I just a lucky fool riding their coattails? And what about the founders who didn't achieve breakthroughs? Were they just unlucky?

MY INNER ANORAK

That's when my inner anorak kicked in. "Anorak" is British slang for a socially inept person with an obsessive-compulsive hobby of tracking arcane subjects the rest of the population would usually find boring. The term comes from train spotters, who frequently wore anorak-style jackets. They would stand outside at train stations for extended periods, regardless of the weather, jotting down the numbers of passing trains.

I'm an incurable anorak. I became obsessed with uncovering the reasons behind why some start-ups achieved extraordinary results while others, despite seemingly following the right steps, struggled or achieved only modest success.

Figuring this out was tough. Start-ups are random and complex by nature. No two start-ups are totally alike. Luckily, I had good relationships with lots of founders. Most would speak honestly with me when I asked. Some had reached greatness, others had suffered failure, and a few had experienced both. I chose my questions carefully, seeking objective truths in their stories.

We are all fooled by randomness in one way or another. Past events always seem less random in hindsight. We can easily underestimate the role of luck in our success and instead overestimate the impact of our abilities or strategies, especially when we've been extremely successful. Taleb believes that many successful people are lucky fools—at the right place at the right time—rather than the skilled geniuses we imagine ourselves to be. Recounting our successes, we combine random events into a pattern that describes a coherent story in which our skill makes us the central figures of our success narrative. By overlooking the role of chance, we miss deeper truths and the opportunity to learn from them.

At the same time, I sensed that there was more to these outcomes than pure chance—that there could be an explanation for why start-up A had a better chance of achieving outlier success than start-up B. I wasn't looking for a magic formula, but I wanted a better understanding of the factors for success. I had to know. I kept digging.

I surveyed our database to pull the successful outliers from the thousands of founders we'd taken meetings with. If we'd rejected the opportunity to invest in an outlier, I reviewed the research work we'd done, the rejection email we'd sent to the founder, and the emails and internal correspondence between me and the rest of the team at Floodgate.

I focused a lot of effort on understanding how founders came up with their ideas. I tried to avoid open-ended questions like "Why do you think this product took off?" because these questions can invite explanations with hindsight bias. Instead, I asked questions like "What motivated you to start building when you did? Did you set out deliberately to build a start-up, or did the idea visit you in a flash of inspiration? What else were you doing at the time? Who were you spending time with to test ideas?"

I asked every founder, "What changed from your first product idea to what it became? What caused you to change course? When was the first moment you started to see things working?"

I searched for unexpected surprises, both positive and negative, eager to decipher their role in shaping success or failure.

I also spent a lot of time trying to learn how founders located their first believers—their early users—as well as the needs of those users and why they had decided to abandon their existing patterns of behavior to embrace something totally new.

All this work was aimed at answering a single question: What was the most important factor that contributed to breakthrough success?

Some days I felt like a lost wanderer, with clarity always slightly out of reach. Still, my research began changing the way I thought about and talked about start-ups. I shared these experiences with students when I made guest appearances at the entrepreneurship course taught by my coauthor, Peter Ziebelman, at the Stanford Graduate School of Business.

Peter said my perspective was strikingly different from that of other guest lecturers. Most speakers emphasized entrepreneurial best practices. They explained how to identify attractive market sectors, how to interview customers to detect their key pain points, and how to create or build a minimum viable product with a defined business model that solves the problem.

In theory, following these best practices seemed logical. Yet looking closer at the founders who tried them, I saw a familiar tale. Despite their meticulous efforts and strong commitment, many failed to achieve their desired impact. The reason? They poured their energies into ideas that appeared promising on the surface but lacked pattern-breaking potential. They didn't have a way to recognize which ideas were worth pursuing in the first place.

Spending more time with Peter's classes, my attention shifted toward the mindset required to birth a pattern-breaking idea. As we pushed our class discussion in this direction, the students' excitement grew. They said it had changed how they thought about testing the power behind their existing ideas and what it might take to build a breakthrough start-up. Peter and I met regularly to wrestle with the questions I was exploring. Slowly, answers began to take shape.

The usual frameworks for understanding why start-ups succeed or fail aren't wrong. They are helpful tools that assist founders in preventing avoidable mistakes. They help a founder adopt proven patterns to be better at the job. People were teaching entrepreneurship like they might teach math or physics or English—like there was a formula or recipe that, when followed correctly, would lead to a right answer.

My research revealed a counterintuitive truth: Founders don't create outlier start-ups by mastering established recipes or best practices. Instead, they embrace pattern-breaking as a core part of their job description and start-up journey. Being extraordinarily different is a key aspect of the breakthrough founder's job description. It's a different type of mindset, one that demands a talent for pattern breaking, an aptitude for breaking the mold.

Interacting with students, we saw the skill, drive, and smarts we look for in founders. Yet if you evaluated their start-up ideas and strategies, they were chasing conventional ideas unworthy of their talents and seemed headed for mediocre success at best.

They were dutifully following the best practices, but it felt like a paint-by-numbers exercise rather than an approach to mastering the art of breakthrough start-ups.

It's even sadder to see a founder try to maintain momentum in a start-up years after realizing it won't make a difference. Driven not by enthusiasm but by obligation, they bear a profound responsibility to family, friends, investors, and employees. Feeling trapped, they waste many of their prime years. This is the real tragedy.

Peter recommended that we give form to the ideas we were developing, a framework to capture the thoughts more precisely. We could offer something new in the conversation of how breakthrough start-ups are created.

This book is written in my voice, but you'll find Peter's influence in every line.

ANOTHER PATTERN IN DISGUISE?

Some of you must be thinking that if we analyze characteristics of breakthrough start-ups, aren't we looking for patterns? And isn't the book trying to propose a pattern for achieving breakthroughs? Isn't that a contradiction?

This is a thoughtful question, and to answer it, I'll concentrate on two key distinctions.

First off, I'm not saying that pattern matching is inherently "bad" or breaking patterns is always "good." They are distinct mindsets, each with benefits and limitations.

Pattern matching is a crucial cognitive skill. It helps us process information efficiently, make decisions, learn, avoid danger, and adapt. It's vital for everyday functioning.

However, these mental shortcuts can also make us miss significant anomalies right in front of us.

Consider a Harvard experiment where students were asked to count basketball passes among players in white shirts. Amidst this, a person in a gorilla suit walked into the frame, lingering for nine seconds while jumping up and waving its arms. Would you have noticed the gorilla in the room? This question provokes a confident "Of course!" from most. Despite this, half the students didn't notice the gorilla. This oversight, highlighted in the book *The Invisible Gorilla*, reveals our perceptual blind spots. It's a clear example of how we overlook the obvious around us.

To achieve a breakthrough, you'll need a different mindset to see what you and others would normally overlook—a pattern-breaking mindset. Discovering breakthrough ideas is challenging, not because they're hidden secrets, but because we're conditioned to notice the familiar, while overlooking what might be.

This leads to the second point: many people look for formulas for success. But the pattern-breaking mindset can't provide a fixed recipe. There's no set of steps guaranteeing a breakthrough; by nature, breakthroughs are undiscovered. Therefore, the concepts in *Pattern Breakers* are not patterns to emulate for guaranteed success. Rather, they are strategies to nurture a mindset that breaks free from conventional thinking and actions. This is different from most business methodologies you'll encounter.

THE PATH TO PATTERN BREAKER

Pattern Breakers will challenge you to rethink why only a select few start-ups transcend the ordinary and achieve the extraordinary.

We first look at how pattern-breaking founders *think* differently: What gives their ideas the power to dismantle the status quo instead of simply enhancing what already exists? Then we turn to how pattern breakers *act* differently: How do they draw the right co-conspirators into their orbit, ignite movements to spread their ideas, and ultimately redefine how people think, feel, and act? Our aim is to distill these insights into practical, actionable steps you can apply directly to your own efforts.

Chapter 1 raises the central questions in *Pattern Breakers*: What nonobvious forces power ideas that upend the status quo? How do pattern-breaking founders succeed at spreading these ideas to other people? When do pattern-breaking principles contradict many of the best practices for start-ups?

In Chapter 2, we show how *inflections* are the underlying force that helps start-ups spark radical change. You will also see, in Chapter 3, how timing is crucially important, and how to turn it into a source of advantage. We'll explore examples of start-up ideas that seemed good but failed because they lacked strong enough inflections to fuel their success.

Having powerful forces behind your start-up idea is necessary, but outlier success demands more. Chapters 4 and 5 describe how your idea also must contain an *insight*. This is a vital element often overlooked by even the best entrepreneurs. Insights provide uniqueness that helps you escape competition. We'll show why a start-up insight needs to be non-consensus and right if it seeks to break patterns.

In Chapters 6 and 7, we emphasize why "living in the future" is the likeliest path to the most powerful insights. We explain the difference between living in the present and living in the future and lay out actionable steps to propel yourself into a future-focused setting. We show you ways to test your insights with potential early believers in Chapters 8 and 9. You'll see why it's vital to seek feedback from those in sync with your core vision while steering clear of people more likely to cling to current norms. We will also help you figure out whether your idea has attracted the necessary enthusiasm among the right circle of early believers to justify the commitment and sacrifices that building a start-up demands. In several chapters, we provide stress tests to challenge whether your concepts truly have the capacity to overturn established patterns.

Next, we move from the concept of pattern-breaking ideas to the decisive pattern-breaking actions necessary to turn those ideas into successes in the real world. In Chapters 10 and 11, we show you how to enlist your co-conspirators—the first true believers who form the heart of your early start-up team, early customers, and initial investors. In Chapter 12, you find your first true believers and start your movement. Chapter 13 describes the importance of effective storytelling to energize your movement. In Chapter 14 we show that for those intent on breaking new ground, being disagreeable is an asset, not a flaw, and how this differs from just being a jerk.

We emphasize in Chapter 15 that pattern-breaking is not just for start-ups; larger companies can apply these concepts to their new products and lines of business. We spotlight companies that have mastered this.

I focus on a handful of start-ups in depth—Lyft, Okta, X/ Twitter, Twitch, and Airbnb—while briefly touching on others. I chose these start-ups for in-depth consideration because I saw them in their rawest form, in the thick of their formative chaos, while they were still grappling with the unknown, well before they achieved the milestones that would propel them to become the household names we know today. Peter and I recognize that we're describing these successful founders and their start-ups as pattern breakers after the fact of their successes. These examples offer not only good stories but also glimpses into the world of those who defy convention. Your path will be different since every pattern-breaking start-up is a unique journey in its own right.

Not everyone views new technology and its creators with hope; skeptics and critics abound. We agree that it is important to see the whole—the excesses in addition to the successes of technology. Yet our demands for such honesty must acknowledge that advances in technology are not just a backdrop to our history; they are a protagonist in it. The mastery of fire, the dawn of agricultural practices, the rise of cities: these aren't just footnotes in our story; they form the very center of human progress. Absent these leaps, our daily lives would be as they were in old times, limited to focusing on our immediate survival needs.

The future doesn't happen to us. It happens because of us. It comes to life when someone dares to supplant old ways with a different way. You will get the most out of these concepts if you embrace the viewpoint of the "unreasonable" person championed by George Bernard Shaw—the mindset of a pattern breaker. Doing so may go against your initial instincts and what your parents, mentors, and well-wishers taught you. That's the magic of it.

Part I

Pattern-Breaking Ideas

*The Counterintuitive Forces That Power
Revolutionary Products*

1

A WAVE OF CLARITY

Introducing Inflection Theory

There is nothing so practical as a good theory.
—Kurt Lewin, pioneer in organizational psychology

One day I was on a surfboard—full disclosure, I'm a terrible surfer—watching the waves roll in, trying to choose one that wouldn't leave me tumbling head over heels. And it hit me. Not the wave, but the clarity I'd been chasing.

There were powerful forces below the surface of a breakthrough start-up idea—forces far more important for start-up success than just the idea itself. Just as surfers need to harness the power of waves, start-ups need to harness the power of these forces to increase their chances of unbounded success. Founders could use these forces to improve their likelihood of overcoming obstacles on the road to extraordinary success. Suddenly, seemingly disconnected aspects of what I was learning began to come together. It was exciting!

INFLECTION CONNECTION

Peter and I call this understanding of the forces that propel pattern-breaking start-ups "inflection theory." The basic idea is this: inflections and insights empower breakthrough start-ups to develop ideas that radically change how people live.

It begins with inflections, which are external events with the potential to significantly alter how people think, feel, and act. Just as a surfer selects the right wave, breakthrough start-ups leverage powerful inflections. An example of an inflection was the introduction of an embedded GPS locator chip in the iPhone 4s in 2011.

A surfer also needs skill to make the most of a great wave. This is where insights come to play, which are ways to connect the power of inflections to a nonobvious way to radically alter human capabilities and behaviors. An example of an insight was the realization by start-ups like Uber and Lyft that the new embedded GPS location capabilities of smartphones could enable people to share their location to allow ridesharing between drivers and passengers. This insight was similar to the way Airbnb had recently made it possible for homeowners to share their houses with guests.

A pattern-breaking idea is a specific product or service based on an insight. In the ridesharing example, this idea is the actual ridesharing app itself. To most of us, set in our ways, these ideas often may seem strange or even nonsensical. They can't be compared with anything that's come before. They don't abide by old rules. They make their own.

Being so distinct, the ideas often draw strong reactions, both positive and negative.

Inflection theory provides a conceptual explanation for why some ideas possess greater breakthrough potential than others. We agree with Kurt Lewin's perspective on the value of a theory: it should offer insights into the mechanism and underlying causes of a phenomenon, align with real-world observations, and guide predictions about what will likely succeed or fail in future situations. Inflection theory aims to help entrepreneurs and investors separate ordinary opportunities from those with the potential to be extraordinary.

Inflection theory departs from the conventional wisdom of first analyzing large markets for unmet customer needs. While initially targeting sizeable markets may seem logical, it rests upon a flawed assumption. It presumes that the primary path to a breakthrough start-up lies in addressing what established companies have failed to provide for their current customers. By adopting this perspective, a start-up unknowingly conforms to the established rules set by existing incumbents in existing markets. The start-up unintentionally forfeits its primary opportunity to create a true breakthrough, which is to deny the very premise of these existing rules.

The real difference between ordinary and extraordinary start-ups is their ability to deliver pattern-breaking products that change the rules rather than simply finding gaps in markets and solutions according to the rules as they are currently defined. Inflections provide the mechanism for start-ups to defy current rules. Inflections help start-ups change the game and the conversation.

Some people use the term "breakthrough" to refer to any company that proves valuable in the long run. We use the term more narrowly. We use it to refer to start-ups that radically change how people think, feel, and act. To understand these start-ups and the forces that empower them to alter the shape of humanity, we need to understand inflections and insights, and their relationship to business ideas. In addition, we need to understand one more thing: movements.

Ideas alone aren't enough for a breakthrough start-up—not even ideas powered by insights and inflections. Founders need to carry people along with them into a radically different future. Founders accomplish this by creating movements that propagate radical change throughout the human population.

Let's talk about each of these points, starting with inflections.

INFLECTIONS

Humans, as noted earlier, are habit-forming creatures. The ways we go about our daily lives tend to crystallize into stable, repeatable patterns. Simple routines like brushing your teeth twice a day as well as more complex social, political, and economic structures are all examples of this human tendency to establish stable patterns of behavior.

But every so often, something happens that disrupts our established ways of being. There's an event that introduces something new—a new technology, a new regulation, a new idea—and that new thing radically changes how people think, feel, and act. Peter and I call this event an inflection.

An inflection is an event that creates the potential for radical change in how people think, feel, and act.

The inclusion of a GPS chip in the iPhone 4s serves as a good example of an inflection. This chip allowed smartphone applications to pinpoint users' locations within one-meter accuracy. Before this change, creating a widespread peer-to-peer ridesharing network would have been nearly impossible, as riders and drivers would have struggled to locate each other precisely. The embedded GPS chip in the iPhone 4s created the potential for radical change, which start-ups like Uber and Lyft capitalized on. With the ability to pinpoint locations accurately, ridesharing networks could allow drivers and riders to effortlessly connect with each other on a massive scale, transforming the way people travel.

Given the current pace of technological change, other inflections are all around us. The cyberpunk author William Gibson says it well: "The future is already here; it's just not evenly distributed." Those pockets of the future distributed unevenly among us are things with the potential to radically change how people live. You could be holding the potential for radical change in the palm of your hand. You could be standing next to it or sitting on it.

Yet most people don't recognize the transformative power of the things they're holding or looking at or sitting on. What prevents them from recognizing the pockets of transformative potential all around them are the patterns of life that they've cultivated over time. The way we habitually engage with recognizable people and objects in our well-known surroundings often hinders our ability to spot new patterns. This familiarity breeds expectation, a kind of inertia. It stops most of us from thinking things could change, from seeing a future where people's thoughts, feelings, and actions are starkly different from the ways they think, feel, and act in the present.

Business is never a fair fight. The default is an unfair fight where the status quo confers an advantage for the incumbent corporate players. It becomes an unfair fight in favor of the start-up when the start-up can change the rules. Unfortunately, most founders are more inclined to build within the current rules, so they never break the pattern.

Occasionally a founder is an outlier, someone who sees the potential for radical change unnoticed by others. This is where insights come into play.

INSIGHTS

An insight is a nonobvious truth about how one or more inflections can be harnessed to radically change human capacities and behaviors.

Many start-up ideas aren't based on insights. Think of a founder who says, "I have an idea: a better security patch update service." This idea isn't based on an insight—at least not in the sense I'm using the term. This idea, even if it's useful, doesn't rely on an insight that harnesses one or more inflections to radically change human capacities and behavior.

Insights are different. They're truths about harnessing inflections to radically change how people think, feel, and act. Even if it's true that people want better ways to manage their software patches, that product idea doesn't have the potential for radical change. At best, it can secure only incremental improvement on an existing product offering. It doesn't expand the range of human capacities or add to the inventory of human behaviors. People were patching their software systems before, and they'll continue engaging in that same activity if they patch their systems in an incrementally improved way thereafter. A start-up in this field can only battle for their share of that market, largely according to the current competitive rules of that market—rules set by formidable incumbents.

By contrast, people didn't tweet before Twitter, a breakthrough start-up that changed the shape of human behavior. We've even had to expand our language to accommodate this change: "tweet" as a verb has a new definition. X/Twitter was based on a real insight—in the same category as transformative inventions like the television, the telephone, the automobile, the rifle, the telescope, the printing press, vaccination, antibiotics, writing, smelting, and cooking.

IDEAS

An insight is a nonobvious truth about the power of one or more inflections to effect radical change. For a breakthrough start-up, an idea grounded in an insight is the necessary next step.

An idea is an attempt to conceive of some specific product or service, based on insights.

This distinction, as well as the connection between ideas and insights, explains why some start-ups but not others achieve unbounded success. Some start-up ideas are based on insights; others aren't. When an idea successfully embodies an insight into a product or service, it harnesses the power of an inflection to radically change how people live. An idea that fails to embody an insight lacks the transformative potential that inflections provide.

The distinction between ideas and insights also helps explain the radical pivots whose origins and success had puzzled me for so long. If you have an insight, your initial idea doesn't have to be right. That idea is just a first attempt at conceptualizing how to embody the power of inflections and insights in a product or service that people can use. That attempt can miss the mark; it can fail to describe a way—or the best way—to embody an insight in a product or service. Figuring out a way—or the best way—to embody an insight and harness an inflection's power might take some experimentation. However many false starts there are, the insight persists while the founder tinkers with the idea, leveraging the ongoing feedback of early believers in their insight. Eventually, the founder co-creates the correct solution with his early believers, based on relentless refinement.

Ideas can miss the mark in two ways. First, as we've seen, some ideas aren't based on insights. Think again of a tool to help people manage their security patches. This idea might seem logical from the standpoint of familiar market evaluations that try to identify trends or pain points or white space, but it is not based on insights, and because of that, its potential upsides are capped.

Why do technology start-ups usually need a distinct insight to maximize their potential? It boils down to how they add value compared to conventional businesses. Start-ups thrive by making rapid, massive strides in value creation, often by disrupting the norm. Instead of outperforming competitors, they redefine the game by introducing entirely new rules based on their unique insights. These insights leverage inflections to deliver transformative changes. While a start-up can achieve success without such insights, doing so is a tougher journey. Without a game-changing idea, a start-up must excel within existing competitive structures, usually gaining only temporary advantages. If competitors see a path to replicating the start-up's idea, they typically will, using existing tactics and capabilities to challenge the new entrant. A start-up with a novel insight disorients traditional competitors by changing the rules and turning the competitor's strengths into weaknesses.

The established company faces a tough choice. Should it compete with the newcomer by the rules of the new pattern—rules that nullify the incumbent's strengths? Or should it wait, hoping the newcomer doesn't dominate future markets and profits?

Take Airbnb as an example. Their fundamental insight was that people would trust booking rooms with locals in the same way they trust booking with hotels. Does this mean no start-up will ever innovate or capture upside in the hotel industry again without an insight? Not necessarily. However, if a start-up launches a new hotel concept and becomes successful, existing hotel giants can likely replicate their innovations and compete, given their expertise in hospitality. In contrast, Airbnb shifted the game entirely. Consider a brand like Four Seasons, which offers a consistent experience globally. Can they suddenly offer a unique, personalized experience in every city without altering their core model? Probably not. This differentiation is what allowed Airbnb to create a new category as it skyrocketed in value, eventually surpassing the combined valuations of major hotel chains like Marriott, Hilton, and InterContinental Hotels Group after its IPO.

Second, some ideas, even if by accident, can have insights below their surface, but they fail to describe a product or service that embodies the insight's real power. Think again about Justin.tv. The key insight was the recognition of people's growing interest in real-time, authentic content and the potential for anyone to become a broadcaster of their own life. This insight flowed from several inflections related to technology, such as a tipping point in the adoption of broadband penetration and the availability of cheap video cameras. The rise of social media platforms was another inflection that portended the public's growing interest in sharing and consuming personal content. This cultural shift toward online sharing made a platform like Justin.tv more acceptable and intriguing to users. The tipping point was highlighted when, just a few months before Justin.tv's launch, Time magazine named YouTube its "person of the year."

The initial business idea—the start-up's first attempt at conceiving of a service that embodied the power of that insight—missed the mark. It turned out that people weren't interested in watching just anybody—whether Justin or someone else—engaging in mundane activities. Rather, people who played video games were interested in watching other people playing video games.

This second kind of failure comes in degrees. There can be better and worse ways of embodying the power of an insight. It's not surprising if your first product idea isn't your best. On the contrary, it would be surprising if your first idea perfectly embodies the power of the insight. It's not surprising if your first product or service idea ends up being substantially different from the product or service you eventually offer. The distinction between ideas and insights also explains why some ideas that initially seemed unoriginal resulted in a breakthrough. However unoriginal those ideas might have seemed, they were based on real insights.

Consider Google. People were using search engines before Google. But before Google, those search engines ranked search results based on keywords. They would, for instance, rank pages by how often a given search term occurred in the page. This approach made sense in theory, but in practice it had major limitations. Suppose, for instance, that I wanted people who typed the keyword "awesome" to come to my website. I could increase the chances of that happening by typing the word "awesome" on my site hundreds of times, even if it was in a color that made it invisible to people viewing it. As a result, I could increase "awesome" traffic to my website even if the viewable content on my page was completely irrelevant to the search's intent.

Google's insight was that a page with a lot of relevant incoming links was likely more valuable to people seeking information about a given keyword. Google thus introduced a new way of ranking web pages based on the connections between them and the directions of those connections. It converted its insight into a powerful idea: a search engine whose results were far more relevant to searchers' interests than those of conventional search engines.

The example of Google shows how people can fail to notice something powerful when they view the world through the lens of the present or limit their assessment of an idea to just the idea, without considering the underlying powers beneath it. When viewed through a conventional lens, Google would have looked like just the latest entry in a crowded search engine market with dozens of competitors. But this assessment reflected a failure of imagination. The people who understood the importance of Google understood that the insight behind Google (PageRank) could create a breakthrough—an innovation that made the product radically superior to what had come before, not just incrementally better.

MOVEMENTS

Ideas based on insights break free from current limits in people's thoughts, feelings, and actions. But ideas by themselves aren't enough for achieving high-impact success—not even ideas based on the most powerful of insights. For ideas to accomplish radical change, founders need to carry other people forward with them into the future they envision. Founders take pattern-breaking actions as they embrace unconventional tactics that move people from the familiar present to an unfamiliar future. They make their desired changes real by leading movements that propagate radical change throughout the population.

A movement is a group of people with a shared belief in moving together toward a different future.

Creating a movement starts with a provocative story that defines a larger purpose—one that extends beyond just the desire of a company to make and sell better products. For example, Tesla's purpose is to accelerate the transition to sustainable energy, not simply to make better cars than Ford or Toyota. That purpose attracts co-conspirators, beginning internally with the members of a team, and then spreading externally to early customers and investors. As more and more people join the cause, the movement takes shape and alters how people in society behave.

As we foreshadowed with the example of Airbnb versus Four Seasons, pattern-breaking movements transform the greatest strengths of incumbent institutions into their greatest weaknesses—the way judo masters use their opponents' size and strength against them. We will explore the details of how this happens in later chapters.

Sometimes, when a movement begins, it spreads like a contagion that can't be stopped. For example, seemingly out of nowhere, OpenAI's launch of ChatGPT reached a hundred million monthly active users two months after its launch; this compares to TikTok's reach of a hundred million in nine months. Such movements sweep across the human landscape and usher in a new future that differs radically from even the recent present. In mere months following OpenAI's launch of DALL·E and ChatGPT, the world's perception of artificial intelligence underwent a seismic shift, evolving more dramatically than it had in all the years before 2022.

Occasionally, incumbents can create movements, for example when Apple introduced the iPhone or when Amazon introduced Amazon Web Services. No matter the size of the company, successful movements deliver the same outcome: they topple the old ways and impose new patterns to replace them.

Just as great ideas are hard to formulate, movements are hard to initiate. The incumbent institutions that dominate the present fight hard against movements—understandably. Their continued dominance—in fact, their continued existence—usually depends on maintaining the status quo. They fight to maintain it using all the powers at their disposal, including the media, lobbying, and lawsuits.

Effective movements require bold, decisive, and sometimes idiosyncratic leadership. Powerful storytelling, briefly mentioned earlier, motivates people to support and champion the cause. Grit, the willingness to choose unconventional methods others might shy away from, and even disagreeableness are often essential when confronting established interests. We'll go deeper into these topics in later chapters.

As movements expand, their impact shifts from influencing a small group to affecting the majority. What was once dismissed or rejected is now embraced as the norm.

WHAT INFLECTION THEORY DOES AND DOESN'T DO

Inflection theory gives us a way of understanding why some ideas are more transformative than others and offer greater upside—in some cases, unbounded upside. It gives us a way of understanding what sets breakthrough start-ups apart from start-ups that achieve only limited success. Once we understand that inflections and insights power breakthrough ideas, and that movements propagate breakthrough changes throughout the population, the difference between a breakthrough and the normal course of either a start-up or an incumbent business starts to make sense. A number of other puzzling phenomena also start to make sense—why, for instance, some ideas that initially seem worthwhile meet with mediocre results, and why others that initially seem unworthy, even idiotic, end up as breakthroughs that radically change how people live.

Neither Peter nor I claim that inflection theory explains every success. Clearly not all business successes—not even all massive ones—involve breakthroughs. A business can achieve massive success for a variety of reasons: It could be that the incumbents are really bad, or that markets are overvalued, or someone buys a company for more than it's worth. A business can also achieve outsized success through financial engineering techniques. For example, roll-ups, where similar companies are merged into a dominant entity, can create value via economies of scale, improved financial metrics, tax advantages, and strategic use of debt.

We also don't claim that inflection theory is a scientific theory, like gravity or relativity. In the philosophy of science, a theory should be framed in such a way that it's possible to disprove it with an empirical observation or experiment. We use the term "theory" in the way Clay Christensen used it when he advanced the notion of "disruptive innovation." His theory explains how a company can start with a simpler, cheaper, or more convenient product aimed at either unserved customers or customers who are "overshot" and no longer want to pay more for increasing performance and capabilities. This theory provides an explanation for why large, successful companies can be overtaken by smaller start-ups, even when incumbents continue to innovate effectively. It offers predictive value to help leaders anticipate potential disruptions to their businesses. And it offers generalization since it applies across different industries and sectors.

We believe that inflection theory provides the best available explanation for an important kind of business success achieved by pattern-breaking start-ups that alter human behaviors. It also helps us identify signals of change on the horizon and how they might be harnessed by start-ups to change the rules. Further, inflection theory provides a framework for founders to stress-test their idea for breakthrough potential. We've observed that it offers generalization in the sense that we have seen inflections power breakthroughs in a variety of unrelated technology fields.

We aren't suggesting that every pattern-breaking founder knowingly applied inflection theory to build their start-ups. People often think a theory comes first and is then applied to produce new inventions. But inventions frequently occur before the theories that can explain them. Steam engines were developed more than a century before the theory of thermodynamics was fully developed. Boomerangs, fermentation, telescopes, gunpowder, antibiotics, balloons, and alloys all were invented before scientific theories came later to explain them. Likewise, business success often precedes the theory that helps us understand its foundations.

We look forward to learning from founders whose triumphs highlight aspects of our theory. We welcome input from those with conflicting experiences and views. Stress-testing our own ideas is the best way to improve them.

Inflection theory provides founders and their co-conspirators (their cofounders, investors, and early customers) a vocabulary for framing their decisions and trade-offs as they move forward. Founders who grasp the theory's elements and rigorously stress-test them will heighten their chances of achieving extraordinary success.

Start-ups require a huge amount of effort and sacrifice. All things considered, most founders we've known would rather pursue ideas that have a higher chance of achieving a breakthrough. But once an idea sets a start-up's direction and the start-up takes flight, it's very hard to turn back. In addition, founders are optimistic by nature. (That's a feature, not a bug.) The cofounder and CEO of Okta, Todd McKinnon, once said to me, "Sometimes you have to believe even when you don't believe." Without commitment like that, founders wouldn't be able to do their jobs. The many obstacles, doubters, and setbacks they encounter would cause them to quit. That's why it's doubly important to know that an idea is worth it before you go all in.

Inflection theory is the best way we've found to test whether an idea is worth the time and sacrifice that founders need to dedicate to the job. Many founders make the mistake of trying to think of a start-up idea and then let their optimism convince them it's an idea worth pursuing. But trying to think of a start-up idea sets founders on a path that relies on the rules of the present. It ends up moving them toward ideas with limited upside instead of opening them up to exploring a new, unbounded future.

Inflection theory can help you determine whether an idea is likely a good use of your time and really worthwhile. It can help identify ideas that seem worthy on the surface but don't contain the underlying powers that suggest it will be a breakthrough. And it can help avoid prematurely dismissing ideas that don't seem worthwhile at first but that have breakthrough potential beneath the surface.

Perhaps you don't have a start-up idea yet. If so, using inflection theory to aid your search is a more powerful starting point than the traditional method of seeking start-up ideas by looking for untapped markets, unaddressed customer needs, or products that cater to those unmet needs. These methods require entrepreneurial skill and contribute to success. Still, they come later—in the same way that skillfully controlling a surfboard comes after identifying which waves are most worthy of catching in the first place.

INFLECTION THEORY TAKEAWAYS

Inflection theory holds that inflections and insights empower breakthrough start-ups to develop ideas that radically change how people live. Here are the theory's key drivers:

1. An inflection is an event that creates the potential for radical change in how people think, feel, and act.
2. An insight is a nonobvious truth about how one or more inflections can be harnessed to change human capacities and behaviors.
3. An idea is an attempt to conceive of some specific product or service based on insights.
4. A movement carries people forward into the future defined by a pattern-breaking start-up. Movements start with the few. They are initially dismissed by most, but eventually the start-up's idea is embraced as a widely accepted truth.

We'll devote the rest of the book to exploring these concepts, beginning with the first and most foundational of them: inflections.

2

HARNESSING INFLECTIONS

How Pattern Breakers Change the Rules

You never change things by fighting the existing reality.
To change something, build a new model that
makes the existing model obsolete.
—BUCKMINSTER FULLER, ENGINEER, ARCHITECT, AND FUTURIST

H ave we ever funded something illegal before?" my Floodgate partner Ann Miura-Ko asked as she poked her head in the doorway. That got my attention.

Ann and I cofounded Floodgate as a venture capital partnership and have worked together for more than fifteen years. The daughter of a rocket scientist, she was a debate champion in high school, graduated from Yale with a degree in electrical engineering, and was five years into her PhD in math modeling of information security at Stanford when we joined forces.

It was the summer of 2012. Ann had returned from a board meeting for Zimride, a San Francisco start-up we'd invested in two years before. Zimride provided a carpooling web hub for college and corporate campuses. It was doing well enough but wasn't setting the world on fire. Now founders Logan Green and John Zimmer wanted to conduct an experiment: a peer-to-peer ridesharing app that ran on smartphones.

But the California state government (at the behest of the taxi lobby) would almost certainly challenge the legality of ridesharing services. Like virtually all major US cities, San Francisco required taxi firms to be licensed according to an old-fashioned medallion system that limited the number of cabs. The city would likely issue cease-and-desist letters to ridesharing services on the grounds that they were unlicensed taxi services.

"Logan and John are going to call it Lyft," Ann continued. "We're putting pink mustaches on the cars so it won't seem as scary getting in a car with a stranger."

You already know where this story is headed. But do you know the route it took to get there? Do you know what transformed the moderately successful Zimride into the spectacularly successful Lyft? Do you know what caused that breakthrough to unfold the way it did?

The answer has to do with inflections, a term that has multiple meanings depending on the context. In speech, it denotes a change in voice pitch. In mathematics, it signifies a point on a curve where the curvature changes direction (see Figure 2.1). I first heard the term applied to business by Andy Grove in the 1990s, when he was the CEO of Intel.

In his book *Only the Paranoid Survive*, Grove described "strategic inflections" as a turning point in the way people think, feel, and

Figure 2.1 In mathematics, the inflection point is where the curve changes direction upward.

act: a change in what they value, what they believe, what they can do, or what they're willing to do. Our perspective of inflections is very similar to Grove's, albeit approached differently. Grove viewed strategic inflections as major threats due to their potential to disrupt the industry's established norms. Companies that failed to identify and adapt to these changes risked becoming irrelevant. The challenge for dominant companies was avoiding complacency and swiftly responding to these shifts. Grove stressed the need for vigilance and adaptability, even suggesting a hint of "paranoia" for continued success amid such changes. His book highlighted instances like the predatory competition in the memory chip market; the internet's reshaping of computing, which shifted the demand for chips and their capabilities; and deregulation in the airline industry, which allowed fare freedom, route choice, and new entrants, leading to pricing wars, efficiency demands, and mergers. In all cases, incumbents who didn't adapt faced potential obsolescence. These inflections usually benefited consumers by increasing access and reducing costs. However, for incumbent businesses, the changes were seen as threats, jeopardizing the market positions they'd long held. Not surprisingly, established leaders often perceive inflections as destabilizing rather than empowering forces.

Peter and I have a different perspective. After all, we work with start-ups—and enjoy it, because they make something out of nothing. They change the future, which means they upend the status quo. From our vantage point, inflections—such as a change in the power of a technology, a change in people's attitudes, a change in regulations—are the underlying force that start-ups can exploit to radically alter how people think, feel, and act and thus create a radically different future.

Consider Lyft and its archrival Uber. Both capitalized on two powerful inflections: the advent of GPS-enabled smartphones that could track location for free, and Facebook Connect, which enabled websites and smartphone apps to incorporate Facebook's profile information, allowing other users to see it. Uber and Lyft exploited these new forms of empowerment in a way that radically changed how people traveled.

An inflection is a type of event—a change. But it's not just any change. It's an underlying change that makes an even greater change possible, one that adds to the inventory of what humans can do. In this way, livestreaming, tweeting, web surfing, and ridesharing all harnessed the power of inflections. None of these activities were possible until an inflection conferred new capacities on people. From a start-up perspective, what makes inflections interesting is that they create an opportunity to alter the rules that govern competition in the future rather than simply improving existing products according to the current rules.

Digital photography is another example. When I graduated from business school in 1994, Apple announced a digital camera called the

QuickTake 100. The initial price was $749. It had no focus or zoom controls and could store eight photos at 640x480 resolution. There was no way to preview images on the camera, and no way to delete individual photos. At the time, Kodak had a $28 billion market valuation and 140,000 employees. The QuickTake 100 did not leave Kodak quaking in its boots. Not surprisingly, it failed to take off.

The digital photography improvement curve climbed at an almost imperceptible rate for a while. It looked like a flat line. But in fact, the technology was improving at an exponential rate off a small base. Then—seemingly overnight—it went nearly vertical in a way that was obvious to just about everyone. Digital cameras as well as the cameras embedded in smartphones became orders of magnitude better for normal people with each passing year. By the time Kodak saw digital photography as a threat, the improvement curve was climbing too steeply for it to respond. This is ironic since Kodak was one of the inventors of digital photography.

The first camera phone was introduced in 1999 with a 0.11-megapixel camera. In 2007, the first iPhone shipped with a 2-megapixel camera. In 2012, the iPhone 5 shipped with 8 megapixels. That same year, Facebook bought Instagram (which had fewer than twenty employees) for a billion dollars, and Kodak declared bankruptcy.

The first digital cameras didn't empower enough people to take the kinds of pictures they wanted because they had such low resolution. By 2012, 8-megapixel resolution was a high enough level of resolution that people would be willing to use them in order to take photographs they cared about.

The advent of new technologies, new regulations, new societal attitudes, new political or economic situations—all of these can be inflections that introduce the potential for radical change. All can be exploited by a start-up, or any organization for that matter. In fact, technology inflections have historically played a pivotal role in shaping political landscapes and influencing political changes, not just upstarts in the business arena. Table 2.1 lists several notable examples.

Table 2.1 Technology Inflections

Printing press (1450s): Johannes Gutenberg's invention rapidly helped spread ideas, leading to the Protestant Reformation and the Renaissance.

Telegraph (nineteenth century): Allowed for rapid communication over long distances, altering diplomatic and military strategies and leading to more interconnected global politics.

Radio and television (twentieth century): Events like the televised debates in 1960 between US presidential nominees Richard Nixon and John F. Kennedy showcased the impact of media on political image.

Internet and World Wide Web (late twentieth century): Public internet standards and protocols opened unparalleled access to information, communication, and connectivity. As a result, they transformed educational and economic opportunities as well as political activism, social networking, and the broader exchange of ideas.

Smartphones (twenty-first century): Smartphones, such as iPhones and Android devices, put advanced, connected technology into the pockets of billions of people worldwide. This led to the emergence of a new app economy that profoundly changed various facets of global society, economy, entertainment, and culture.

Artificial intelligence (twenty-first century): Large language models have significantly enhanced AI's capability to comprehend, interpret, and produce human language. Services like ChatGPT have created new opportunities for millions of people in writing text, brainstorming ideas, and even developing computer code, greatly increasing efficiency and creative output.

Many of the examples we use to illustrate the power of inflections come from technology since that is where we have been most active as investors and co-conspirators. But the importance of inflections extends beyond technology to society-wide attitudes and new political or economic situations. Table 2.2 offers examples.

Table 2.2 Societal and Political Inflections

American Revolution (1775–1783): Led to US independence from Britain and the establishment of a republic.

Industrial Revolution (beginning in the late eighteenth century): A transformation that fueled the growth of cities, changed social structures, and set the stage for modern capitalism and industrial policies.

Bolshevik Revolution (1917): Led to the rise of the Soviet Union and the spread of communism as a major world ideology.

Fall of the Berlin Wall (1989): Marked the beginning of the end for the Soviet Union and the Cold War.

Global Financial Crisis (2007–2008): A financial crisis that had a massive impact on the world economy and led to major political and economic shifts worldwide, including greater scrutiny and regulation of financial markets.

Brexit (2016): The United Kingdom decided through a referendum to exit the European Union, resulting in economic shifts, adjustments in laws and regulations, and signaling an increase in populism and nationalism across the West.

While we respect the role of societal and regulatory inflections, it's still technology that dominates the reshaping of human capabilities. Things surrounding us daily might not scream "tech." But dig a bit, and you'll see that technology likely pushed them forward at the start. Take something simple, like the cereal you eat for breakfast. In the late nineteenth century, when John and Will Kellogg invented a cereal that had a long shelf life, it was a major technology breakthrough. Most significant progress, from conjuring fire out of the darkness in ancient times to the use of movable type in the Middle Ages to tapping into artificial intelligence today, comes from mastering and applying new technologies. This is why Peter and I prioritize technology inflections as a necessary ingredient when evaluating new start-up ideas.

That said, we frequently observe how technological changes can intersect with political, societal, or regulatory shifts to enhance their collective impact. Outside the realm of start-ups, inflections can influence any organization's potential to spark significant transformation. Individuals in any organization—be it a budding enterprise, established business, political group, or nonprofit—should monitor inflections for their transformative potential. Recognizing inflections can be a powerful tool for challenging and reshaping the status quo in any domain. Not every new thing marks an inflection, and neither does every widespread societal change. Consider fads or crazes. They're not inflections even if they're widespread, because they don't radically expand human abilities. Fidget spinners, cronuts, and avocado toast didn't add to the inventory of radically new things that humans can do. Fads and crazes are just new expressions of well-established commercial patterns.

THE UNFAIR ADVANTAGE

Inflections aren't caused by start-ups. They happen externally to start-ups. That's one of the reasons that the radical success of some start-ups and the failures of others puzzled me for so long. Returning to the example of content streaming, how did Justin.tv, initially perceived as a poorly conceived venture with limited funds and an inexperienced team, pivot to become Twitch, a streaming powerhouse?

In contrast, why did the streaming start-up Quibi, with its massive funding and pedigreed team, fail so completely? Quibi was a mobile-focused streaming service that offered premium on-the-go video content lasting ten minutes or less. It featured shows across various genres: drama, reality, comedy, and news. Led by Jeffrey Katzenberg and CEO Meg Whitman, Quibi boasted $1.75 billion in funding and a massive investment in content from celebrity A-listers. Yet it shut down in October of 2020, barely six months after launching. Quibi failed for the same reason any new product fails: They didn't offer something unique enough that people desperately wanted, and customers didn't want to add another streaming subscription fee when they were often paying for several already. Many of the platform's social features were poorly conceived, and it only worked on mobile devices. But numerous products miss the mark at first and iterate to correct their initial mistakes, particularly when lots of capital is available.

Quibi's decision to give up so quickly is better understood by its failure to harness inflections. At its heart, Quibi's strategy rested on a seemingly pivotal moment: the confluence of mobile-first viewing, microentertainment, interactivity, and social media clout. Yet by 2020 this wasn't a new frontier, but rather a well-trodden path. Giants like Netflix, Hulu, Disney+, and Amazon Prime had already made their marks, and then there were the tech-centric offerings, like Twitch and YouTube. Quibi's foray into the short-content realm was akin to the latecomer at a party—not exactly crashing it, but certainly not the guest of honor. Its attempt at differentiation was lost amid a crowd of already entrenched alternatives. Investing heavily in marketing and star-studded content wasn't enough for Quibi to gain attention. It wasn't just about having a voice; it was about having something singularly compelling to say. Without tapping into an inflection, Quibi had nothing to say that would make it stand out. Its problem was more profound than missteps in execution; the idea itself was a fundamental miscalculation. Instead of becoming a groundbreaking force that reshaped our media appetites, Quibi was predestined to be a cautionary tale. To the founders' credit, they quickly grasped this reality. Rather than delaying the inevitable, they chose to wind down operations and return the remaining capital to investors.

Comparing Justin.tv/Twitch to Quibi underscores another key distinction about inflections we previously mentioned: They aren't mere trends, business drivers, or progress curves. Instead, they're specific change events that mark pivotal shifts, enabling radically new capabilities that didn't previously exist. While the emergence of short-form content is an important trend, it's only an inflection if it can offer something revolutionary that wasn't possible before. Merely adopting a popular trend doesn't equate to capitalizing on an inflection.

Twitch's success versus Quibi's failure highlights the difference between tapping into inflections versus merely following trends. An inflection offers a chance to radically change human capabilities for the first time. In Twitch's case, home broadband had recently advanced to a stage where high-definition video streaming was accessible to most people. Multiplayer games designed for replayability had concurrently seen a surge in popularity. This pivotal moment, marked by the capability to widely stream games just as they were becoming popular shared experiences, allowed Twitch to launch something new and compelling that gamers hadn't seen before. Twitch's livestreaming service tapped into the growing gaming culture and offered a unique, interactive, and community-driven platform for both viewers and streamers. In contrast, when Quibi launched its short-form, mobile-centric streaming service nine years after Twitch, mobile media, streaming, and short-form video had become commonplace. Quibi's inability to identify and capitalize on a new inflection meant it didn't introduce anything that seemed radically different. Customers quickly lost interest.

Using inflections gives start-ups an unfair advantage—and they need it. Big companies have employees, customers, supply chains, competitive moats, an established reputation or brand, and many other assets a start-up lacks. Ultimately, an incumbent's biggest advantage may be that they benefit from people's established patterns of behavior.

A start-up's advantage, by contrast, depends on redefining people's patterns of behavior—on replacing established patterns with new ones. As creatures of habit, humans get entrenched in ways that gain inertia over time. Overcoming that inertia takes something powerful—an inflection. That means inflections are the start-up's most important opportunity to make a major impact.

Why do so many start-ups fail to harness the power of inflections to radically change the future? Why do they miss the wave? The answer is that many start-up founders begin by looking for trends in the here and now, or for big markets with white space and pain points. As a result, they fail to discover inflections that can help them transcend the status quo.

Many start-up presentations fail to pinpoint a transformative inflection that can power a fundamental breakthrough, even though they offer details about a problem and a seemingly fitting solution. Take climate change, for instance: while numerous pitches target problems in areas like electrified transportation or decarbonization, few tap into a significant inflection to address the problems. When I ask something like "Can you help me understand the inflections that are happening outside your start-up that have enabled you to do this just now?" I often get a blank look. I've learned to recognize this as a sign that the start-up solves an incremental problem in the present instead of offering a breakthrough with the potential to radically change the future.

Founders might reference advancements in battery efficiency or declining green energy costs, but too often they emphasize the gradual progress of a technology curve rather than the tipping points that could usher in revolutionary products and alter customer behaviors.

It's insufficient to just observe that solar energy costs are dropping by 7 percent each year. That's a powerful trend, but lots of people know about it. More importantly, it doesn't show a turning point that can alter human capabilities. Recall our earlier example of Instagram. The digital camera improvement curve represented the ongoing increase of megapixels in smartphone cameras. The inflection was the turning point when smartphone cameras became good enough for people to want to share their photos broadly. The improvement in cellular network speeds simultaneously reached an inflection, surpassing the threshold of making it easy to upload those higher-res pictures quickly. Returning to solar energy, an inflection should demonstrate how solar technology improvements are on the verge of providing new capabilities that were once nearly possible but can now be fully realized to benefit people at scale. Despite the challenge, I'm still optimistic about potential breakthroughs in solar and climate change in general. I want to meet founders who see an inflection coming and understand how it will empower people at scale.

Breakthrough start-ups use the power of inflections to create a new game with new rules that they define. They force a choice and not a comparison. They can't be reconciled with the offerings that came before. That's how they change the future.

While technology improvement curves are not the same as inflections, the two have an important relationship. A technology improvement curve is like a mountain range whose summits represent pivotal points along the way. The summits are inflections-defined moments that provide the ability to empower people with radical new capabilities. The most famous example of an improvement curve is Moore's Law, formulated by Gordon Moore, the cofounder of Intel, which states that the number of transistors on a microchip will double roughly every twenty-four months at a given price. This curve has persisted as a constant force enabling change for decades. It has catalyzed multiple inflections through time. It made personal computers possible in the first place. As performance improvements marched on, they begat future inflections that enabled graphical user interfaces, smartphones, and later cameras that were of high enough quality to enable photosharing apps on phones. In all these cases, the continued march of technology improvements created new tipping points along the way that exceeded the threshold that may enable a pattern-breaking innovation.

With such exponential improvement, new empowerment changes emerged on the horizon: the milestone of graphical screens with windowing interfaces, phones that slipped into our pockets but held the world, and embedded digital cameras that reached a point where sharing life's moments became a spontaneous act. Moore's Law hasn't only enabled consistent technological growth; it has also led to significant milestones where inflections enabled innovators to develop products that were radically different from previous offerings.

As a technology improves at a faster rate, it tends to lead to major advancements more frequently. Rapid progress up the technology curve means big changes happen more often and more quickly. For example, between 2009 and 2019, the cost to produce electricity from solar panels dropped by 89 percent. This means performance doubled roughly every 38 months and saw a tenfold increase about every 126 months. Consider again Moore's Law: performance of microprocessors doubles every twenty-four months and multiplies tenfold around every eighty months. Then there's Huang's Law, an observation by NVIDIA's cofounder and CEO Jensen Huang that the performance of graphics processing units (GPUs) doubles about every fifteen months and experiences a tenfold boost every fifty months. This is especially exciting for the AI field since GPUs drive most advancements there. Genome sequencing is advancing even faster, with performance doubling almost every eleven months and growing tenfold approximately every thirty-seven months. See Table 2.3 for a summary of these improvements.

Table 2.3 Pace of Technological Improvements		
	Time to 2x improvement in performance (months)	Time to 10x improvement in performance (months)
Solar panels	38	126
Microprocessors	24	80
Graphics processing units (GPUs)	15	50
Genome sequencing	11	37

It's crucial for founders to assess the technologies they're working with and how fast they are advancing. The pace of this advancement significantly influences their chances of shaping the near future. In areas like genomics and AI, numerous opportunities for major shifts are on the horizon. However, for those focusing on solar panel advancements, it's vital to pinpoint when and how these improvements will lead to groundbreaking change. They might also consider pairing a potential future shift with other, faster-evolving technologies that can offer inflections sooner. After all, creating a transformative impact becomes more challenging if the potential for change takes longer to materialize and is harder to foresee within a specific time frame.

Similarly, an inflection is likely to be more powerful if the pace of its adoption accelerates at a more rapid rate. When smartphone penetration exceeded Microsoft Windows penetration, that was a critical moment, because it meant a massive shift in how corporations spent their IT budgets. Until that moment, when Microsoft shipped a new Windows version, people upgraded reflexively. But with that change, smartphones became the center of the action.

This dynamic applies when multiple inflections overlap—like the constructive reinforcement of superpositioned waves. Improvements in smartphone camera resolution made impromptu photos look better, but they need more storage. Cellular network operators constantly improve their networks with the ability to move picture data more quickly. Instagram benefited from these improvements in the cellular data infrastructure that made it quicker and easier to upload higher-quality photos. Kodak could have taken advantage of these same inflections to dominate digital photography. They did not.

THE INFLECTIONS STRESS TEST

When I meet founders, they usually have an idea in mind. As you might suspect, I often ask whether their idea taps into one or more inflections. More specifically, I try to determine:

1. Have they connected a specific and powerful change from the outside world to the opportunity to empower people with something they never imagined possible?
2. Who are the people this capability would empower, and why would they desperately want the new capabilities?
3. Under what circumstances might the inflection significantly change people's lives, and when might it not be impactful enough?

Table 2.4 offers a simple stress test for these three components.

Table 2.4 Inflections Stress Test	
Inflection	**Inflection description**
The new thing	The specific new thing introduced What it enables
Why it's powerful	The magnitude of the empowerment The people who are affected by the new empowerment
Conditions for success	Factors outside the start-up's control that can help the inflection achieve its full potential

By applying this stress test, you can decide whether to move forward with confidence that your idea has underpinnings powerful enough to offer breakthrough potential. (In later chapters, we will apply this stress-test approach to insights and other aspects of assessing a start-up's opportunity to create a pattern-breaking idea.)

For founders who are in search of an idea, starting with inflections—rather than trying to think of a start-up—will increase their chances of landing on an idea with the potential to create radical change.

In Table 2.5, we apply the stress-test method to one of the inflections that powered Lyft and, for that matter, Uber: the advent of GPS-enabled smartphones that could track drivers' and riders' locations for free.

Notice how this example of the GPS smartphone offers specific detail about the components of an inflection. It describes in a concise way the inflection along with what it enables. It also describes the specific way the inflection empowers people and the relevant set of people who could be empowered. Finally, it outlines

Table 2.5 Inflections Stress Test: GPS-Enabled Smartphones	
Inflection	Introduction of iPhone 4s with embedded GPS chips
The new thing	The iPhone 4s was introduced with highly accurate, embedded GPS chips that enabled smartphones to be reliably located within one-meter accuracy.
Why it's powerful	For the first time, apps could locate smartphones precisely and algorithmically via application programming interfaces (APIs). Earlier smartphones contained location services that were far less accurate. Given the explosive adoption and rapid replacement cycle of smartphones, this change could impact tens of millions of smartphone owners in the short term and almost all of them in the long run.
Conditions for success	For this inflection to fulfill its potential: • enough people would need to have smartphones with these capabilities soon; • these capabilities would need to persist in future smartphones; • people would need to be willing to share their location information with applications harnessing this power.

the conditions for success—a concept that merits further elaboration. Founders harnessing inflections are placing bets on whether their chosen inflections can radically change the future. But the future hasn't happened yet, and it's highly uncertain. This requires us to embrace a mindset of "thinking in bets," which involves carefully evaluating the conditions that could make an inflection transformative, as well as recognizing situations in which it may not make a substantial difference.

In her book, *Thinking in Bets*, author and former professional poker player Annie Duke effectively conveys this approach. She suggests that in the face of an unpredictable future, we should treat decision-making like placing a bet—carefully weighing the probabilities, uncertainties, and the spectrum of possible results.

When it comes to inflections, defining the conditions for success helps us assess their likelihood. As the future unfolds, what signals would suggest we were right about the bet we made on the conditions for success, and what signals would suggest it is not going our way? Anticipating the answers enables us to react decisively as events unfold, whether our bets on an inflection are working for us, against us, or somewhere in between.

For Lyft and Uber, the pivotal inflection bet was on the quick adoption of smartphones with built-in GPS and whether users would be comfortable sharing their location data with app creators. These bets paid off. But things don't always break your way as a founder, even if you're right about the power of the underlying technology. Various factors can inhibit people's knowledge or willingness to embrace the empowering capabilities of a new inflection, including regulation, social stigma, cost, and other issues. Nuclear energy, for instance, empowers people to consume cheap, reliable energy while also decreasing carbon emissions. Over the past fifty years, regulatory hurdles, public opinion, political factions, and other issues have prevented its empowering conditions from being fully met.

Under the right circumstances, though, regulations can change—even producing an inflection of their own. A good example is the new telehealth regulations introduced in response to the COVID-19 pandemic. See Table 2.6 for an example of an inflections stress test for telemedicine.

Table 2.6 Inflections Stress Test: Telemedicine	
Inflection	**Introduction of pandemic-era telehealth regulations**
The new thing	The COVID-19 virus required people to shelter in place, which resulted in new regulations that allowed telemedicine visits to be reimbursed by medical plans and be conducted across state lines.
Why it's powerful	This empowered patients and doctors because it facilitated more choice and better economics for both, potentially impacting the majority of patients and doctors in the United States.
Conditions for success	For this inflection to fulfill its potential: • enough patients need to continue to want to have a meaningful share of their visits occur remotely; • enough doctors need to continue to want remote visits as well; • regulators need to allow patients and doctors to exercise their preferences; • the standard of care for remote visits relative to in-person visits needs to be good enough to justify them after things return to normal; • the new regulation needs to persist after the pandemic ends.

3

TIMING IS EVERYTHING

One of the Dumbest Ideas Ever
and How It Broke Through

My belief has always been that timing is the
major variable. It's the major form of entrepreneurial
risk in the tech industry, and I think maybe by a
wide margin.
—MARC ANDREESSEN, VENTURE CAPITALIST,
INNOVATOR, AND CREATOR

We've defined an inflection as a change that a start-up can exploit to radically alter how people think, feel, and act. We've also suggested that exploiting an inflection's potential to change the future requires combining the new thing with people's willingness to exercise the new power it gives them—and that brings us to the importance of timing.

The arc of technological improvement is ever present. But there are limited windows in time in which an improvement reaches a tipping point in its ability to effect change. You may have correctly identified an inflection, but if you act too quickly to harness it, you've got a science project. It's too soon to radically change human behavior. If you act too slowly, you've got what is now a conventional idea, embraced only after it became obvious to many others—leaving your idea to compete against a crowded field. There's a Goldilocks moment, neither too early nor too late but just right, when you can bring about meaningful change.

Of the numerous risks you face, timing is perhaps the biggest, and it is fraught with the most uncertainty. Here's just one example: Ironically, many of the ideas that formed the foundation of the iPhone were tried over a decade earlier at a company called General Magic, which was staffed with some of Apple's earliest and most prominent technical leaders. But the technology wasn't yet ready to enable the right capabilities at the right price to achieve the type of revolutionary success the iPhone enjoyed. In another ironic twist, many people from General Magic came back to Apple, ready for the right moment for the iPhone to become a phenomenal success.

Conventional thinkers often maintain that if something was tried in the past and didn't work, then it's already been "proven" not to work. This betrays a lack of understanding of how inflections drive change. It has never been easier to start a company or launch a new product or service. The world of start-ups is efficient at letting every idea get tried. The key question to ask isn't whether an idea has been tried before; it probably has. The important question is: Why is now the time it's going to work? What inflection has emerged that makes this time different? Quite often the team that finally gets the timing of an idea right isn't even aware that it's been tried before and failed—and that's to their advantage. You can think of it this way: Every breakthrough will happen. The question is when, not if.

When a venture capitalist responds to your pitch by asking, "Why now?" they're really asking, "What inflections does your idea harness? And why is now the time to harness them?"

TIMING, TAKE TWO:
INFLECTIONS AFTER YOU START

Start-ups often benefit from inflections that occur after they start. Remember, Lyft didn't begin as Lyft. It started as Zimride, a web-based hub that enabled commuters to share rides at corporate and college campuses. John and Logan launched the Lyft service after the inflection of the iPhone 4s, with its introduction of embedded GPS-locator chips.

Zimride was based on a different inflection: the Facebook Connect third-party application programming interfaces (APIs). In fact, Zimride received a grant from Facebook because it intended to use those capabilities. Table 3.1 shows how a stress test of the Facebook Connect inflection might have looked in retrospect.

One reason Ann and I backed Zimride in 2010 was because of what we had learned from our foolish decision to pass on Airbnb in 2008. At the time we heard the Airbnb pitch, we thought, "Nobody is going to want to stay in a stranger's house. That's crazy!" But the launch of Facebook Connect not long after we passed had a big impact on Airbnb's prospects. People seemed far more familiar if hosts and guests could see each other's Facebook profile information.

Table 3.1 Inflections Stress Test: Facebook Connect	
Inflection	**Introduction of Facebook Connect third-party APIs**
The new thing	Facebook introduced Facebook Connect third-party APIs to developers in 2009. The new service enabled people to learn about other people's identities from their Facebook profile information.
Why it's powerful	It allowed people to confidently interact with others who might have been strangers before. It also allowed them to rate each other and have those ratings attached to their social identity. Since almost everyone has a profile on Facebook, this development potentially impacted nearly anyone with a computer or smartphone.
Conditions for success	For this inflection to fulfill its potential: • Facebook needed to continue to make the Facebook Connect API available or not radically change the cost of harnessing it; • people needed to be more trusting of strangers if they could see their Facebook identity—as was the case with Airbnb.

The iPhone 4s was introduced later, in 2012. This inflection made it possible to offer ridesharing for everyone, at the level of peer to peer. The Zimride founders were savvy enough to grasp that fact quickly. The Uber team came from a different starting point, since they had developed a premium service for black-car drivers and riders, but they were similarly tuned in to the potential of this new inflection. The two companies noticed it at the same moment and ultimately pivoted to ridesharing services that put them in competition in the same new market.

X/Twitter offers another example. It was launched before Apple introduced the iPhone and the App Store. But as soon as those new inflections arrived, X/Twitter's opportunity expanded because it became far easier to compose tweets on mobile devices at any time. The new inflection was a force multiplier for X/Twitter's already compelling opportunity.

GOOD IDEAS, BAD IDEAS—AND BREAKTHROUGHS

An inflections stress test can help a founder weed out some of the most dangerous ideas of all: plausibly good ideas that aren't driven by any sort of inflection. Because these ideas sound plausible, most people you talk to about them will think they make sense and should be launched. The false positive of that feedback can reinforce your own intuition and lead you to devote years of your life to an idea with limited upside. As an example, I've often been pitched on ideas related to mental health. The founder will say we're in a mental health crisis, it's gotten worse with the pandemic or Instagram, it's having a huge negative impact on society, and we've got to do something about it. I agree! A new idea to better address mental health will generate a lot of positive feedback. People have personal experiences that will help them relate to the idea. They may get very positive encouragement from investors, advisers, and others touched by a mental health crisis. Despite the encouragement, the idea needs to be supported by an inflection that offers a set of empowering capabilities to change the future of mental health.

An inflections stress test can also protect the seemingly bad idea because of the powerful underlying inflections it reveals. That's part of what's so humbling about start-ups: many of the very best ideas seem bad but turn out to be non-consensus and right.

Let's go back to the beginning of my business relationship with Justin Kan and what became Twitch. On the surface, nothing about it suggested breakthrough success in the making.

I was wrapping up a pitch meeting in Palo Alto one day in 2007 when a stranger walked in. For a moment he stood silhouetted in the doorway like a character from a 1950s gunslinger movie. But it was a coffee shop, not a saloon, and he wore a hoodie instead of chaps and a baseball cap instead of a cowboy hat. Attached to the cap was a camera with wires running into a backpack. Even by the standards of Silicon Valley, this was all a little weird. He began walking straight for our table as if he'd come to meet me.

Which he had.

I'd been talking with the founders of Weebly, a start-up that made it easy to build websites. I told them that I wanted to invest and would talk with other people I knew who might join me. And now here came this guy, whom they'd invited to crash our meeting. They'd alerted me by email not long before we met, but I hadn't seen the message. It still makes me smile when I look back on it.

"He's got this new idea called Justin.tv," the Weebly guys said. "We think you're going to like it. Do you have time to let him explain it?"

"I guess I do now," I said, as our new guest sat down next to me and took out a laptop.

"My name is Justin Kan," he said, "and I'm with a start-up called Justin.tv. I'm going to create the internet's first livestreaming reality show where viewers follow me throughout my life twenty-four/seven." He turned the laptop toward me. An image of my face filled the screen because he was live-casting me as we talked.

I tried to be as delicate as possible, but it wasn't easy. "Justin. Come on. That's one of the dumbest business ideas I've ever heard." I meant it. It really was—hands down—one of the dumbest business ideas I'd ever heard. Still is.

But there was something different about Justin. He came across as someone who liked to kick ass and make things happen. Plus, the technology worked, which was no small thing. "How does it get from the camera on your baseball cap to the screen?" I asked. "What's in the backpack?"

"The internet is a hostile networking environment," he explained. "It's very difficult to stream video live." (Remember, it was 2007.) "But we've put together some hardware that's based on the cellular network combined with software that's native to the internet. That allows us to stream live. We believe that content delivery networks are going to get better in the next few years, and that will make it much easier for everyone to stream live video. By then we'll have a big lead."

I wasn't thinking then in the language I'd use now, but Justin had just touched on a potential inflection lurking beneath his crazy idea.

Intrigued, I went home and set out to learn a bit more about Justin and his team. It turned out that he and another Justin.tv cofounder, Emmett Shear, had already started a company that made an online calendar system called Kiko. Then Google came out with its online calendar and gave it away. Game over.

Normally when people sell their company, they try to think of another company that might acquire it; maybe they'd pitch it to Google or Yahoo or eBay. But Justin and Emmett put Kiko for sale on eBay. No one does that! In fact, no one even thinks of doing that. But they did—and they sold it for $250,000. I loved that!

I decided that if anybody was going to figure out livestreaming, it might just be Justin and his team. They had the technical talent, the passion, and the frugality to spend the absolute minimum required to build a business. That very night, I decided to cut them a small check and see what happened.

I've already told you how the story ended: over the next seven years, what started as Justin.tv became Twitch, the world's dominant livestreaming platform for gamers. Justin and his cofounders created a new form of social activity. In 2021, 22.8 billion hours of live content were streamed on Twitch.

How could an idea as dumb as Justin.tv end up transforming entertainment? The answer has a lot to do with inflections. Video streaming had started working at scale with YouTube beginning in 2005, and by 2007 broadband penetration had become extremely high. Those inflections were obvious by the time I met Justin. The key question to ask in evaluating Justin.tv wasn't whether anyone would watch his life all day and all night. It was whether content delivery networks had reached an inflection point that would enable livestreaming.

That's why the contents of Justin's backpack that day were so important: he and his cofounders were employing a clever use of EVDO (evolution-data optimized) cellular technology combined with internet streaming software. This apparatus allowed Justin to capture video live from anywhere with a cellular connection (basically anywhere) and stream it to the internet for viewing via a browser. I could also see that CDNs, or content delivery networks, were improving at a rapid rate. I thought this would continue and further enhance the opportunity to livestream at a higher quality and lower cost in the future.

In addition, user-generated content was becoming a big deal in blogging as well as on news sites like Digg. The Time magazine person of the year in 2006 was "you," a takeoff on YouTube, which had been a runaway success. The trend was clear: people wanted to express themselves through these newly emerging platforms, and video was at the center of it all. Why wouldn't they want to stream live videos too?

Justin.tv launched as nothing more than a twenty-four/seven livestream of Justin's daily activities. Its novelty didn't attract much attention. But not long after I invested, the team made their first pivot. They dropped the Justin reality show and relaunched as a platform, segmented by channels, where anyone could broadcast their own live videos. The pivot created a new set of issues because people started streaming copyrighted live content, such as sporting events. (This development landed another Justin.tv cofounder, Michael Seibel, in front of a congressional committee, whose members were not too happy about this use.) The founders pushed their way to profitability by running ads, but they weren't doing anything they thought was destined to truly matter. It felt like they were wasting their time.

The inflections were real, but something was still missing. Another Justin.tv cofounder, Emmett Shear, began losing faith. He dialed back for a couple months, didn't work as hard, hung out with friends, and played video games. Paradoxically, the act of letting go opened his mind and brought him closer to a breakthrough idea.

Emmett asked himself a simple question: How do I actually use our own platform? The answer was also simple: he liked watching skilled people play video games. He wasn't alone. About

2 percent of users did the same—and it was a passionate 2 percent. Emmett did some digging. He asked about forty gamers why they livestreamed themselves in action and what could make the experience better. It seemed like a small opportunity, but one worth exploring, so Emmett and his team created more appealing features for gamers to stream as well as a way for them to make money off their streams.

More people began coming to the site. "It started feeling more like you were chasing a boulder down a hill than you were pushing a boulder up a hill," Emmett later said. "We really started getting this sense of pull, where the market was pulling us along."

Twitch.tv was officially launched as a separate entity from Justin.tv in June 2011. It featured video game livestreaming, esports competitions, personal player streams, and gaming talk shows. Today, Spencer, my gaming and media-savvy son, still considers Twitch the best idea I ever supported.

INFLECTION FAILURE MODES

While success stories afford insight into understanding how inflections can drive success, equally critical to understand are four pitfalls that can lead you astray. The first is a lack of clarity about what constitutes a specific change event. Many people have ideas about opportunities presented by technologies that are improving rapidly. I'm often pitched by people who describe the accelerating improvements in the cost of sequencing DNA. I agree that such improvements are significant and will most likely continue. But an improvement curve is not the same as a turning point that introduces something specific and new. Earlier we pointed out that the inflection behind the popularity of Instagram was not just the improvement in digital photography. The key inflection was a tipping point in the number of high-quality cameras in people's hands. They could take a high-quality picture at any time and share it with a friend.

When Microsoft was started back in 1975, many people, especially in technology, understood Moore's Law, which, as described earlier, states that the number of transistors on a computer chip at a given cost would double about every two years, increasing the speed and capability of computers. But Microsoft was formed as a response to a very specific change event: the introduction of the MITS Altair personal computer. The MITS Altair was a specific new thing: the first commercially successful personal computer. Microsoft's product, called Altair BASIC, was a programming language that allowed hobbyists to write computer programs on their personal computing device.

The second possible pitfall is not understanding the empowerment offered by an inflection, who it affects, and the extent of its impact. Climate change is one example. An aspiring founder might say, "The world has decided it's time to do something about the climate crisis. It's now in the popular consciousness. People are ready to change their behaviors and buying habits." My natural tendency is to say, "I agree with that sentiment. Now, let's connect that with a new thing that empowers people in a specific new way. And further, let's get clearer on why it can confer those powers on lots of people rather than just a few."

The third pitfall is becoming attached to "being right" about how an inflection will play out in the future. It is more important to have a thesis stating the conditions that are required for the inflection to have an impact—and under what conditions that impact might not be realized.

The fourth pitfall, and the biggest mistake I see, is a lack of specificity. In pitches, I often hear assertions like "The cloud changes everything" or "AI is going to change the rules." Both statements might be true—but they need to be more specific. As general statements, they're not useful.

MORE INFLECTION TAKEAWAYS

As we dive further into inflections, here are four additional points to keep in mind:

1. Be careful about ideas that sound good but are not grounded in powerful inflections. An inflection is the asymmetric weapon that powers a breakthrough, creating a different future. Don't settle. If your idea is not grounded in a powerful inflection, that is a warning sign to think more deeply about what makes the idea powerful, or to question whether it is sufficiently powerful to be worthy of your time and sacrifice.

2. Do not rush to reject ideas that sound crazy at first; they may be great ideas that tap into powerful inflections. We will talk more about pivots in future chapters, but it's important to remember that powerful inflections at the core of an idea retain their power, even if the ideas themselves change. Given a choice, I would prefer to start with a seemingly bad or ambiguous idea powered

by strong inflections than a plausibly good or seemingly straightforward idea where I can't identify an underlying set of inflections that are powerful enough to create radical change. The first option is still risky, but it usually has better odds of success and certainly better odds of achieving outlier success.

3. Be skeptical when someone says it's been tried before and didn't work. Over twenty-three thousand start-ups raised seed funding from 2016 to 2020, a sevenfold increase from the prior decade. Chances are, someone has already explored any idea you come up with. Yet whether your idea has been tried isn't what really matters. The more important question is why is now the time for the idea to work, as opposed to the past. If you can point to a specific inflection that makes it different this time, you might be on to an important insight that others dismiss when they fail to evaluate your idea beneath the surface. For example, a lot of people thought Instacart could not work because Webvan had been a flameout just a decade earlier.

4. Stress-test your ideas by considering their underlying inflections in sufficient detail. Thinking about inflections in depth leads you to consider a series of critical questions. What is the specific new thing that has happened? How does it empower people, and whom does it have the potential to empower now and in the future? And under what conditions might your idea be too early, too late, or just right?

For all their power, though, inflections aren't enough to produce radical change by themselves. Their potential needs to be unleashed by a founder who has an *insight* about how to harness them. But what is an insight, exactly, and how do you come up with one? How does an insight relate to inflections? This is the topic we will turn to next.

4

DIFFERENT IS . . . DIFFERENT

She Gave Me That "You've Gone off the Rails Again" Look

In order to be irreplaceable, one must always be different.
—COCO CHANEL, FASHION DESIGNER

I tend to fall irrationally in love with ideas, and quickly. My Floodgate cofounder, Ann, is more skeptical. In Floodgate's early days, we almost always sat in on entrepreneur presentations together. As fate would have it, one of the first was a pitch from a cereal company called Mojo Mix. You'd specify your own personal ingredients for a cereal made just for you, place the order online, and Mojo Mix would blend the components and send the result to you in a custom box.

Ann wasn't impressed. "Why did we even take this meeting?!" she said later. "We invest in tech start-ups, not cereal."

I protested. "I think it's cool!" (I like almost everything, after all.)

"Who cares if it's cool or not?" Ann replied. "That's not what we're paid to invest in!"

I had to concede the point. Begrudgingly.

A couple of weeks later, in July 2008, Ann and I met with Brian Chesky, Joe Gebbia, and Nate Blecharczyk, the founders of AirBed and Breakfast. We walked into the conference room, where I was surprised to see . . . cereal boxes. Stacked everywhere. But these were not cereal boxes like you would find in a supermarket. They were labeled "Obama O's" or "Cap'n McCain's," and all were made by hand.

Ann gave me that "you've gone off the rails again" look. She didn't have to say it out loud. I could read it in her expression: "Another cereal company? What the hell?!"

"Maybe I'm confused here," I said to Brian. "I thought this was AirBed and Breakfast."

"It is," said Brian, "but we haven't raised money from investors yet, so we've been selling these cereal boxes. People are really excited by the upcoming election campaign between Barack Obama and John McCain. And they have the added benefit of drawing attention to the fact that it's going to be impossible to get a hotel room at the Democratic Convention, which is coming soon. Do you want to buy one?"

I declined. (That was my first mistake: they're collector's items now. But it gets worse.) We were there on account of a Justin.tv cofounder, Michael Seibel, who had introduced me to Brian. Brian referred to Michael as the "godfounder," which I must confess made me grin, because Michael was only three years out of college himself. Michael had been advising Brian from almost the very beginning, even before Brian had applied to the accelerator Y

Combinator.* The fact that Michael asked me to meet with Brian before Y Combinator was telling. It meant that Brian's team hadn't fully baked their idea and pitch yet. But Michael had prepped Brian well, emphasizing my affection for product demos over pitch decks. I've always preferred seeing the real thing, not slides. These product demos reveal the source of the founders' excitement, what they have figured out, and what they haven't.

Each investor has a preferred method for evaluating start-ups. While many rely on slide presentations to understand the team, market, and progress, I place a higher value on product demos, at least initially. These demos bring a start-up's vision to life by providing a tangible mock-up for early customers—and investors! Nothing compares to feeling the raw, unbridled excitement founders radiate when they share their creations. When I experience firsthand a team showcase their product, I gain an unobscured view into their passion, priorities, and vision. The demo illuminates what they believe truly matters and what can wait. More crucially, it exposes whether they've really tuned in to creating something people will be desperate for, rather than debating about what they might someday build. Slides, on the other hand, barely scratch the surface of revealing this dynamism.

"We thought we'd show you our product," Brian said, and proceeded to bring up their website.

---

* Founded by Paul Graham, Y Combinator put start-up accelerator programs on the map, providing a ten-week bootcamp that put founding teams through a rigorous process to help them get their ideas in shape and launch something. Paul vetted the applicants to the program and gave the founders he selected a stipend so they could support themselves as they tested their ideas to see if they might turn into real companies.

Now we're talking, I thought.

Nothing. It wouldn't load. We all know the feeling. It happens.

"That's fine," I said. "No big deal. Let's just go through your deck."

Crickets.

We all looked at each other until Brian confessed, "We didn't bring one. We wanted to show you the product."

"Okay," I said, "Let's just talk about it."

"What you do," Brian said, "is you stay at somebody's house. They give you an airbed to sleep on, and the next morning they give you breakfast. AirBed and Breakfast. It's going to be valuable in places where they have unpredictable patterns of hotel occupancy, like Denver hosting the Democratic Convention. There aren't any hotel rooms left there. We're going to blow up at the convention." Fortunately, I understood Millennial-speak and realized that would be a good thing.

The idea of staying in a stranger's house made me a bit nervous. "How do you know someone won't get murdered in one of these houses?"

"It's all about trust. We're going to have a rating system."

"Isn't there already a site called Couchsurfing.com?" I asked. "It raised a bunch of money, but it really hasn't really gone anywhere, and it's free. Why is somebody going to pay money for AirBed and Breakfast when there's already a free version?"

"Trust matters more than price," Brian said.

"Okay, but why are they going to trust you more than they trust this other company?"

"We're going to have a rating system on our platform."

This is the part of the conversation where I went wrong. Brian saw something profound: the opportunity to apply ratings and reviews to lodging and hospitality.

In the fledgling days of the internet, pioneering start-ups like Amazon faced a critical challenge: they were unknown entities in the eyes of consumers. Handing over a credit card felt daunting. How could I know that Amazon would really ship me a book and not steal my credit card info? It became evident that the traditional approach, where companies cultivated trust by building brands over many decades, would be too slow for internet start-ups. The answer lay in the immediate feedback loop provided by ratings and reviews from fellow customers, which became a new digital-native currency of trust.

In our discussions, Brian understood that online couchsurfing offerings had missed something important: finding lodging wasn't purely about cost. The challenge lay in establishing trust. How do you convince someone to trust a host who doesn't have the brand reputation of Hilton or Four Seasons? Brian, having grown up during the internet revolution, lived under different assumptions. His generation of digital natives viewed the internet as an integral fabric of their lives. Their experience of technology was inherently different. By the time AirBed and Breakfast (now known as Airbnb) emerged on the scene, ratings and reviews were no longer novel for someone of his cohort; they were expected. Brian recognized an opportunity to extend the established feedback system of ratings and reviews used in e-commerce to build trust in lodging and hospitality.

In spite of how discombobulated the meeting had been—the cereal boxes we were predisposed to dislike, the demo that didn't work, the slide deck they didn't bring—it was still kind of interesting. Brian and Joe had graduated from Rhode Island School of Design. Nate had received his computer science degree from Harvard. But lots of founders I encounter show the markers of conventional success. Brian had an X factor. Beyond his achievements, there was an undeniable charisma about him, a draw that made you want to root for him. He had an innate flair for telling fun and engaging stories. He seemed like someone you'd enjoy getting into trouble with. Beyond these traits, he showed an impressive openness to unorthodox strategies. Few founders would think to fund their ventures by selling cereal boxes. Even fewer would boldly imagine and pursue the idea of people welcoming strangers into their private spaces: their homes.

There was another key element I overlooked. Seated quietly in that room was Airbnb's understated cofounder, Nate Blecharczyk. Nate epitomized what we at Floodgate now call a superbuilder. A superbuilder is someone endowed with not just technical prowess but also insatiable curiosity, unwavering tenacity, and a staunch belief in their capability to surmount any technical hurdle. Such individuals, I've observed, are often a linchpin in start-ups that achieve outsized success.

As Airbnb's trajectory unfolded, the company would grapple with an array of giant technical challenges: scaling its platform to accommodate millions of users, navigating the labyrinth of payment processing, instilling robust systems for host and guest identity verification to foster trust, and safeguarding their review mechanism from potential manipulations, to name just a few.

The very unpredictability of these types of challenges on the path to hypergrowth makes superbuilders incredibly valuable. They stand ready not just for the challenges they foresee but for the unforeseen ones that the future inevitably holds. Embedding such capability in a start-up's founding team gives them a huge unfair advantage, because it means the team can tackle any unforeseen technical challenge that might arise down the road. Even though their demo tanked, Nate turned out to be someone who can build anything. I had been too distracted to probe exactly what he brought to the table, which was another mistake.

In the chaos of the meeting, I failed to see the signal in the noise. On the surface, the pitch felt chaotic and screwed up. Brian Chesky even mentions it as his worst pitch ever in *The Airbnb Story*, the definitive account of the company's rise. I ended up passing; I didn't invest. It's still my biggest miss.

So what, exactly, did I overlook?

Brian grew up a digital native, very comfortable with ratings and reviews. Their potential to build trust among strangers was the insight at the heart of Airbnb's massive success. (The "airbed" and the "breakfast" parts later fell by the wayside, which would become another factor in their success: their ability to actively listen and tinker with new iterations.) Brian's vantage point enabled him to grasp the power of ratings to create trust among strangers in a digital age, just as brands had created trust by different means in the industrial economy. His reasoning about establishing trust wasn't circular at all; it just seemed so obvious to him that he didn't bother explaining it. And I was so distracted by the other stuff in the meeting that I wasn't focused enough to ask him my favorite question these days when I'm skeptical: "Can you say more?"

On the surface, it seemed Brian's idea had been tried before—and not only that, Couchsurfing.com was free. But to think of AirBed and Breakfast as another couch-surfing deal was to make the mistake of fixating on the idea without adequately exploring the insight and inflections below its surface.

Brian's insight was that online trust techniques can substitute for people's trust in hotel brands. And this insight was reflected directly in the business idea in terms of the rating system, professional photos, and strict attention to detail around all customer concerns related to trust. Because I had compared the ideas at a surface level, I missed this key difference. If I'd had inflection theory at my disposal, that's a mistake I might have avoided. (At least, I try to convince myself of that.) Fortunately, Brian didn't let my mistake slow him down in the least! Airbnb became one of the most impactful new companies of the decade.

Developing a compelling insight is one of the most important parts of the job description for a breakthrough founder. So, then, what is an insight? Why do they matter? Where do they come from? What can you do to increase the chance of developing one that leads to a breakthrough?

WHAT IS AN INSIGHT?

We've talked about the power of inflections and how founders can harness them to overturn the assumptions of the status quo. But inflections on their own are not enough. Equally important if not more so is converting the potential of an inflection into a product that changes how people will think, feel, and act in the future. The insight is what connects the two; without an insight, the inflections that surround you will not be harnessed effectively to create a breakthrough.

An insight is a nonobvious truth about how to harness one or more inflections to change human capacities or behaviors in a radical way.

Insights are important because the presence of a powerful new technology doesn't guarantee that it will be used to maximum effect. Consider the wheel, which existed for hundreds of years before it was used for transportation. For all those centuries, people simply mounted wheels horizontally to streamline pottery making. Let's give the Mesopotamians their due. After all, before the pottery wheel, pots were made from strands of clay that were rolled into long threads and manually coiled. The use of the wheel for pottery was therefore an insight as well. But for the wheel to realize its potential as we understand it today, someone needed to have a second insight: that the wheel could also be mounted vertically to enable transportation.

The example of the wheel shows that just because you have a power doesn't mean you know you have it or know how to use it. This is what makes some inflections so interesting, especially from a business perspective. Most people don't know that new powers are now available for them to harness. They don't recognize that a new thing has appeared in their environment that empowers them to do things they've never done before. As a result, they continue with business as usual, unaware that the power to create radical change is there for the taking.

Some founders have the insight to see these powers and harness them to create radical change. The insight behind Uber and Lyft was that it is possible to apply the sharing economy to cars. Just as Airbnb had allowed people to share an extra room in their houses, ridesharing start-ups like Uber and Lyft proposed to let people share an extra seat in their cars. It was possible, in other words, to radically change how people traveled from one place to another through an app that harnessed the power of GPS-enabled smartphones together with people's willingness to share their location.

THE UNFAIR ADVANTAGE

Inflections, as we explained in the previous chapter, aren't caused by start-ups; rather, they are external events. Insights are different. They come from the minds of start-up founders who see what others don't yet see. So, then, why are insights so crucial to breakthroughs?

Andy Rachleff, cofounder of leading venture capital firm Benchmark and CEO of Wealthfront, offers my favorite explanation. Rachleff applied a brilliant investment theory from prominent investor and writer Howard Marks to the world of entrepreneurship. Start-up ideas can be placed in a two-by-two matrix, as illustrated in Figure 4.1.

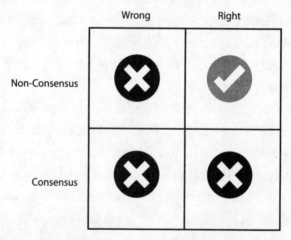

Figure 4.1 An insight must be non-consensus and right to have pattern-breaking potential.

It's probably obvious that if you are wrong, you will not build something people want. So you fail. But it also turns out that being right is not enough when it comes to creating a pattern-breaking start-up. You have to be right and non-consensus.

Here's why. If you are right but within the consensus, you will likely encounter lots of obstacles: new competitors, pricing pressure, longer sales cycles, faster retaliation from incumbents, and many other factors that can all contribute to arbitraging your profits away. A good example in recent years was the mindless competition we witnessed between the scooter start-ups. Companies like Bird, Lime, and more than a dozen others raced to flood cities with their electric scooters, leading to oversaturation in many markets, backlash from city governments, and piles of abandoned scooters heaped up on the sides of roads. Not surprisingly, this type of competitive pressure made profits almost nonexistent.

Being non-consensus and right is the path with the highest odds of achieving a breakthrough. But it's an emotionally harder path to follow. It requires you to break free from the herd and resist the temptation to imitate others. Because your insight is non-consensus, it requires you to acknowledge that most people won't like your insight at first. After all, if too many people like it right away, it's too similar to what they already believe, which makes it unlikely that your insight is different enough—or even an insight at all.

Being non-consensus and right provides many more benefits: it lets the start-up compete based on being different, rather than being better. Think about it. If an incumbent product exists and you enter the market and say you are better, why should anyone believe you? The incumbent has been in business for a while. They have a lot more resources than you. They have more proof points of making customers successful.

But different is . . . different. It's more believable from a start-up because you are not comparing yourself to what is already in the market.

The power of different favors the start-up because it forces a choice and not a comparison. Suppose incumbent companies sell apples. As a breakthrough start-up, you don't want to offer a five-times-better apple. You would be better off saying, "I have an entirely new thing: the world's first and only banana." Not everyone will want your bananas. But 100 percent of the people who do want them will only be able to get them from you.

This example may seem overly simplistic, so let's consider real examples of technology breakthroughs. When Apple introduced the iPhone, people didn't ask, "How does that compare to the BlackBerry?" When OpenAI introduced ChatGPT, people didn't ask, "How does that compare to Google Search?" And when Tesla introduced the Model S, people didn't ask, "How does that compare to a Mercedes?" All these products escaped the comparison trap by forcing a choice, not a comparison.

Being different also gives you time to test, iterate, and learn from early customers and the market before competitors enter. Think of the baby wildebeests born on the Serengeti plains. They fall to the ground in a wet sack and have only a few minutes to get up, find their footing, and start to run. Those who can't are quickly surrounded by jackals, hyenas, Nubian vultures, and worse. When you are a start-up, it helps to have time to find your footing without the pressure of incumbents immediately deciding to attack you. You don't have a lot of people and resources. You are vulnerable. Being non-consensus affords extra protection from the hostile elements in a world where people don't yet really care what you are doing. If they're aware of your start-up at all, most think it's unimportant because they haven't discovered the power of your insight to effect radical change.

The role of insights has clarified for me why some start-ups with great-sounding ideas or solid execution can still fail while others achieve breakthrough success despite many apparent missteps. For unconventional success, start-ups need to create something *unique* that people are *desperate* for. Together, inflections and insights are mutual multipliers—inflections create the conditions for radical empowerment, and insights create the conditions for radical differentiation. When it comes to start-ups, better doesn't matter. Customers won't embrace a start-up's product or service because it's marginally better; ideally, the product must offer something completely different that customers desperately want and can't get elsewhere. A compelling insight that harnesses inflections is vital for standout success.

Let's dig deeper into Lyft's inflections and connect them to the founders' insight and how the founders created a multiplier effect between the two. As an inflection, the launch of the iPhone 4s with embedded GPS locator chips was instrumental. It ushered in an era where apps could algorithmically pinpoint anyone with such a smartphone. Building on this, another significant development was Facebook Connect, which allowed users to share their social identity outside Facebook.

These shifts transpired irrespective of whether Uber or Lyft capitalized on them. The brilliance of ridesharing was in discerning that the concept Airbnb had championed in the housing sector—home sharing—could now be applied to transportation. The founders' insight was rooted in the belief that individuals would be open to sharing rides with strangers, both as drivers and as passengers. If there was a silver lining to our foolish decision to pass on Airbnb, it was that it prepared us to be more receptive to Lyft's insight.

The inflections underpinning Uber and Lyft were not just minor; they were transformative. Their insight to apply those powerful advances to ridesharing acted as a multiplier effect. When you intertwine potent technological advancements with groundbreaking insights about how to harness them, the outcome is often transformative products that redefine industries. Before the new, foundational capabilities, nobody could have created a ridesharing network in the sense we understand them today. However, once those inflections were accessible, the insight uncovered by Uber and Lyft allowed them to usher in a service distinct from anything preceding it. Once passengers tried a ridesharing app, few found themselves drawing parallels with traditional taxis. The ridesharing networks redefined the playing field, aligning it with their unique strengths.

Start-ups, as we've emphasized, need an unfair advantage because incumbents benefit from people's established patterns of behavior. A start-up's advantage, by contrast, depends on breaking people's patterns of behavior—on replacing established patterns with new ones. The first weapon a start-up needs, then, is an inflection that exists external to any business but creates the initial conditions for radical change. Subsequently, insights are internal. They convert the opportunities posed by inflections into a potential breakthrough that impacts people in a way that radically alters the future.

Why do so many fail to get there? A key reason is that many start-up founders begin by looking for underserved markets and unmet customer needs. They then feel compelled to immediately create a product that meets market demands and customer needs in the here and now. But, in doing so, founders frequently skip the crucial step of determining if their idea embodies an inflection and an insight. As a result, they come up with an idea that does not offer compelling enough value (because it lacks an inflection with sufficient empowering capabilities) or enough differentiation (because it does not rely on a unique insight). As a result, they often miss out on the opportunity to pursue an idea with pattern-breaking potential.

More likely than not, what they've really done is identify a consensus opportunity. As of this writing, AI is changing art. AI technology inflections like large language models (the deep-learning algorithms that use very large datasets) make it possible to create incredible art in a way that's empowering and exciting. Suppose you want to create a start-up that harnesses these inflections. The problem you'll face is that many see this change and will be quick to jump in. The trick is to be different, to think beyond the obvious. If you do what a lot of other people end up doing, you'll get lost in the comparison trap. Users will benefit from your creation, but your business risks becoming a replaceable commodity in an endless competitive race.

Another example of the perils of the comparison trap can be seen in the market for meal-kit delivery services. Start-ups like Blue Apron, HelloFresh, Sun Basket, and others entered the space around the same time. A lot of customers liked the products they offered, but the insight behind preassembling meals in packages to be delivered was not very novel. This sector experienced high customer acquisition costs, low customer loyalty, and significant logistical challenges. None of these companies were able to clearly dominate, and many faced financial struggles.

Suppose you've identified a powerful insight that aligns with major inflections. How do you stress-test your insights to confirm if you are non-consensus and right? This is the area we'll concentrate on next.

5

STRESS-TESTING YOUR INSIGHTS

How Valid Is Your Insight?

*The third-rate mind is only happy when it is thinking
with the majority. A second-rate mind is only happy
when it is thinking with the minority. A first-rate
mind is only happy when it is thinking.*
—A. A. MILNE, AUTHOR, *WINNIE THE POOH*

Our definition of an insight—a nonobvious truth about how a start-up can harness one or more inflections to change human capacities or behaviors in a radical way—suggests four tests to determine whether you have an insight.

First, insights must be truths. Falsehoods don't count. You know that two plus two cannot equal five. So, an "insight" that two plus two equals five is obviously false and a nonstarter.

Second, insights cannot be obvious. Obvious truths don't count either. It is true that many customers are interested in an AI co-pilot for the products they use everyday. For instance, an AI co-pilot interface for Microsoft Excel might be very valuable for users, but it's not an insight because Microsoft is already highly likely to implement such a feature. This makes sense intuitively. Most big problems in the present have been solved or have big companies focused on solving them in the near future.

Lots of people deeply explore the territory of the obvious because it's so easy for them to locate. Breakthrough ideas, however, come from exploring the unknown terrains of the future and discovering things that are likely to radically change how people live. This requires founders to live in a radically different future. The more radically the future differs from the present, the more radically it departs from the ways people currently live, and therefore the less obvious the truths about that future are likely to be.

Product ideas based on obvious truths have either a limited upside or a high likelihood of failure. Consider the example of the AI co-pilot for Microsoft Excel. Because this is obvious, it's already well known by established incumbents. They have far more resources to devote to solving the problem than a start-up, and they actually ship the products that contain the capabilities. If a start-up tries to compete, it's likely to lose—unless its founders have an insight that yields a new pattern of behavior rather than a "better mousetrap" that leads to incremental improvement. You want to avoid the trap of competition from incumbent companies or other start-ups. The more obvious your idea, the more likely it is that you will fall into the comparison trap and secure limited upside at best, failure at worst.

Third, insights must harness the power of inflections. Non-obvious truths that fail to harness the power of inflections are not insights. The insights we care about harness one or more inflections to change human capacities or behaviors in a radical way. Gimmicky or meme-worthy ideas that are trendy but that don't result in a sustainable change in how people think, feel, and act don't count as insights as we think of them. A good example is the company Groupon, whose name is a combination of the words "group" and "coupon." It provides daily discounts on local goods, services, and experiences. From half-priced massages and resort stays to deals on classes, medical services, and local attractions, Groupon taps into a wide spectrum of offerings.

Groupon catapulted into the spotlight, boldly rejecting a $6 billion acquisition offer from Google and going public soon after in 2011 with a $17.8 billion valuation. Yet over the past ten years, its fortunes have seen an equally steep decline. By early 2023, its value had tumbled to $103 million, a staggering drop from its initial public market debut.

Groupon's primary issue was its transient novelty, which attracted attention for its bold claims but failed to offer sustainable value. The allure of daily deals was their fleeting availability, urging consumers to act fast. However, as users became accustomed to the bombardment of deals, the excitement dwindled. For businesses, the discounts combined with Groupon's cut made profitability challenging. Ultimately, instead of solidifying as a behavior shift for consumers and businesses, Groupon's model faded due to oversaturation and unmet promises.

A pattern-breaking idea must transcend fleeting attention. It should offer a transformative empowerment that stands the test of time, replacing existing norms. At its core, this requires an insight about how to harness inflections that have the potential to create a valuable and sustainable new form of empowerment that's durable and lasts beyond the initial novelty.

Fourth, insights should answer the question "Why now?" There is a limited time window where an improvement reaches a tipping point to effect radical change that is the foundation for your new idea. Insights, when they are well articulated, have an embedded answer to the question "Why now?" Why is now the right time to introduce this idea?

As with inflections, we suggest in Table 5.1 a simple stress test for the components of an insight.

Table 5.1 Insight Stress Test	
Insight	Insight name
In the future . . .	A new thing Who it empowers How it empowers
This new thing will be enabled by . . .	A named, specific list of inflections
This future is non-consensus because . . .	The barriers presented by the status quo to this happening
But the insight is right because . . .	Hypothesis about how the inflections and insight will prove the status quo wrong
And the timing is right because . . .	Statement answering "why now?"

Airbnb highlights an idea born from necessity that leads to an insight. In 2007, Joe Gebbia risked losing his San Francisco apartment when his roommates left, and he couldn't afford the rent. He persuaded Brian Chesky to move from LA and live with him, despite

Brian having only $1,100 in his bank account. They needed to find ways to quickly get more money. Seeking an immediate answer, they brainstormed alternatives. One idea zeroed in on a four-day industrial design conference that was coming to town. Gebbia figured, why not turn the empty space in their apartment into a bed-and-breakfast for the conference? The event was sure to draw a few thousand designers to San Francisco. The city would soon be swamped with new visitors. Hotels would fill up fast and room rates would be higher than usual.

They'd offer each guest an air mattress, internet access, a space to work, and Pop-Tarts for breakfast every morning. They hired a freelancer to design a WordPress-based website and marketed it as "It's like Craigslist & Couchsurfing.com, but classier." They were surprised to learn that the conference organizers and design blogs were happy to promote them, and within a few days they had already booked three guests.

It could have stopped there—but it didn't. Brian began asking questions that simply hadn't occurred to others, and he dug deep for answers. Where did travelers stay before there were hotels? How did hotels come to be? Why did travelers trust them? And what did travelers do when hotels were all booked?

Brian drew on another distinct advantage that shaped his viewpoint: he was among the first of a generation of digital-native leaders.

Those born before the early 1980s, including Baby Boomers and Gen Xers, can be thought of as "analog natives." For them, technology was a layer added to their daily existence, with computers seen as tools augmenting their real-world interactions. Analog natives today represent roughly 136.8 million Americans.

Conversely, digital natives, spanning younger Gen Xers to Millennials, grew up immersed in technology. Their upbringing embedded technology into every facet of their lives, leading them to place high value on their digital identities and experiences. Life was no longer supplemented by technology; the digital domain became the primary place many of these people spent their lives. Recent data indicate that digital natives now make up the majority of the US population.

When Airbnb was in its infancy, digital natives were a distinct minority. Within this minority, fewer still were at an age to start breakthrough businesses. As early leaders in this cohort, people like Brian Chesky and Mark Zuckerberg benefited from a distinct perspective compared to most business contemporaries at the time. Brian's digital-native worldview made him more attuned to recognizing the potential of building trust through online peer reviews and ratings combined with professional photos. His product choices resonated strongly with other digital natives, the early adopters of Airbnb, much like Mark Zuckerberg's decisions had with the initial users of Facebook. The financial crisis of 2008–2009 hit digital natives like Brian especially hard. As recent college graduates, many faced significant debt, experienced financial challenges, or were outright broke. People were desperate for ways to generate income during the Great Recession, ideally by leveraging what they already owned (or, in Brian's case, rented). In addition, online commerce had reached a tipping point.

All this led Brian, Joe, and their Airbnb cofounders to their insight: ratings and reviews could build trust among strangers to create an entirely new category of hospitality. Instead of focusing on sold-out conferences, Airbnb very rapidly became a website that made booking a room in someone's house as convenient as booking a hotel room. And in many cases, it was a superior alternative. You can go to a Hilton anywhere in the world and have a great experience, but every Hilton is the same.

Suddenly, you could rent someone's house or apartment—and have a genuinely local experience that often was less expensive than a hotel. Airbnb created a new kind of democratized "solopreneur" ecosystem, allowing anyone who owned property to become an entrepreneur and monetize it. Airbnb changed people's idea of travel. The Airbnb founders were not just digital natives who understood the changing online habits of people in their demographic; they were also Millennials, a cohort whose members were known for valuing artisanal experiences over corporate-branded ones. Their generation, empowered by the vast and competing information on the internet, grew skeptical of traditional advertising and the intentions of big corporations, often perceived as faceless. They gravitated toward genuine, transparent brands and experiences. This was evident in the rise of farm-to-table restaurants, handcrafted goods on platforms like Etsy, craft breweries, and independent coffee shops.

When traveling, Millennials prioritized immersive, local experiences over typical tourist activities. They valued the stories and community connections that artisanal products offered, allowing them to showcase their individuality in contrast to the image imparted by common, mass-produced items. Growing up amid the 2008 financial crisis also made them value-conscious, seeking meaningful experiences that offered genuine value for the money they spent.

Airbnb realized that people, especially Millennials with a digital-native perspective, would trust booking houses and apartments with locals just as much as they trusted established hotel brands—if users could combine online trust with a more artisanal experience. They also realized that many travelers were shifting their focus from central commercial hubs, where most hotels were located, to more residential and authentic parts of cities. Instead of staying in a typical hotel in a city's business district, travelers now craved the experience of residing in a quaint area like Beacon Hill in Boston or a medieval villa in Provence.

Table 5.2 shows how Airbnb's insight fares in a stress test.

Table 5.2 Insight Stress Test: Airbnb	
Insight	People will trust that they can book rooms with locals, in the same way they trust booking with hotels.
In the future . . .	People will be able to book rooms with locals.
	Travelers will find this empowering both because price is an important concern, and because hotels leave you disconnected from a city and its culture.
	Hosts will find it empowering because it will be a new way for them to make money.
This new thing will be enabled by . . .	Facebook Connect third-party APIs, which allow people to interact with others who would have been strangers before personal information was available.
	Online ratings and reviews, which are increasingly becoming an acceptable substitute for the type of trust that requires a mainstream brand.
	The 2008 financial crisis, which created a strong desire for travelers to save money and for property owners to find new ways to make money and pay for their existing mortgages.
This future is non-consensus because . . .	Most people think staying in a stranger's house is unsafe.

But the insight is right because . . .	The inflections we've described will overcome the trust barrier for both renters and hosts.
And the timing is right because . . .	Ratings and reviews have been gathering steam. The introduction of Facebook Connect, combined with the financial crisis, will create the conditions for this new way of booking rooms to take hold.

We can look at Lyft through a stress test to understand the insight behind the inflections: Facebook Connect third-party APIs along with the introduction of the iPhone 4s and its highly accurate GPS locator chips. See Table 5.3 for the Lyft insight stress test example.

Table 5.3 Insight Stress Test: Lyft	
Insight	**Riders will trust that they can get a ride with a stranger just as they trust getting into a taxi.**
In the future . . .	Ridesharing networks will allow anyone to catch a ride anywhere almost instantly via a smartphone app.
This new thing will be enabled by . . .	The new chips embedded in the iPhone 4s, which detect locations within one-meter accuracy. Social reviews. Facebook Connect profile info.
This future is non-consensus because . . .	Most people think riding in a stranger's car is unsafe.
But the insight is right because . . .	Most people underestimate the power of the inflections we described to overcome the trust barrier. Plus, Airbnb is already beginning to prove that people will stay in a stranger's house or apartment.
And the timing is right because . . .	Social reviews and Facebook Connect are already gathering steam. The accurate GPS chips complete the availability of enabling technology for all riders and drivers to locate each other.

INSIGHTS AND TIMING

Timing, as we saw earlier in the chapter on inflections, is an important determinant in the potential to create a breakthrough. Insights take this a step further. The most powerful insights harness inflections that have already been established and combine them with inflections that are new to create something radically different. In the case of Airbnb, ratings and reviews were already gaining traction as a mainstream way for people to build trust online, beginning with sites like eBay and Amazon. And Facebook Connect provided the enabling technology to facilitate new levels of trust that overcame the concern people had about staying in a stranger's home. In the case of Lyft, Airbnb had shown that Facebook Connect could be leveraged to create trust among strangers, but the iPhone 4s provided the enabling technology to complement this with the ability for riders and drivers to locate each other accurately and in real time. In both cases, the founders had to grasp the implications of the new inflections and how to harness them to create a nonobvious insight about the future that had become imminently possible.

Which of today's developments capture my interest the most? How could they connect to insights into what's coming next?

Improvements in deep learning, big data, hardware acceleration, cloud computing, transformers, and large language models have converged in a perfect storm for a massive AI platform shift, paving the way for remarkable new products. OpenAI's ChatGPT has exploded, gaining a hundred million users in two months. AI will change virtually everything that matters in the private and public sectors. It will soon reshape policies, ethics, and the very fabric of society.

Climate change has been a discussion topic for decades, but we see a shift in thinking as an ever-increasing number of people have witnessed the effects firsthand with raging fires and more frequent flooding.

Not surprisingly, I find these developments very exciting, and I'm not alone. In 2022, the fervor led to a surge in AI start-up investments exceeding $50 billion. AI's potential is compared to earlier technology sea changes, like the PC, the internet, and smartphones. Start-ups face big challenges to create a breakthrough using AI when viewed through the lens of the importance of insights. They cannot just rely on the allure of new technology.

First, start-ups are pitted against dominant incumbents like Google, Microsoft, and OpenAI, who have extensive financial, data, and infrastructural resources. These giants possess the vast proprietary datasets vital to AI's data-intensive processes, robust infrastructure to implement AI solutions at scale, an established market presence, experienced technical talent, and the ability to attract some of the very best.

Start-ups also fight hard against each other. Exciting AI innovations quickly become commonplace because AI methods can be replicated easily, and new findings are swiftly integrated into products, especially with the prevalence of open-source projects. The high demand for a limited pool of the most talented AI experts intensifies the competitive environment. These challenges make it hard for start-ups to maintain their edge.

Which start-ups will form a non-consensus insight that differentiates them from both established companies and fellow start-ups? How could such an insight enable some to have the impact that past upstarts Microsoft, Google, Amazon, and

Facebook once had? Merely sharing the excitement that many others feel isn't sufficient. For start-ups seeking exceptional success, discovering a unique insight will be essential. If you have one, you now know whom to stress-test it with!

INSIGHT FAILURE MODES

One common pitfall is to conflate the belief that your idea is missing from the world with the belief that you've discovered an insight. The improved security patch management idea, while perhaps better at addressing a potential customer need than what exists today, isn't powered by a fundamental insight. Customers wanting to better manage their security patches is an idea for an improved product rather than an insight about the future.

Failure also takes place when a perceived insight about the future is wrong. This might seem like a rookie mistake, but it happens frequently. I have a great deal of sympathy because consensus ideas are easy to validate quickly. Non-consensus ideas, on the other hand, are harder to prove right away, by their very nature. The challenge of pattern-breaking entrepreneurship is that in the beginning, you don't truly know if you are non-consensus and right. Most often you find out first that you are non-consensus, and then only later, after taking the upfront risk that you might be wrong, do you validate that you are right. In my view, it's still better to risk failure on this dimension than to cap your upside from day one by pursuing something that's consensus. In today's landscape, for example, AI ventures seem to attract capital with remarkable ease, even when the ideas will also attract dozens of competitors. But just because you can raise money for such ideas doesn't mean that you should. The genuine quest is for enduring truth rather than fleeting affirmation. Often, the popular consensus gravitates toward notions that, even if valid, offer restricted upside because what seems like an initial advantage can get arbitraged away by excessive competition.

A third failure mode is to pursue an insight that the status quo has the power to defeat, often unfairly or with nonmarket forces. I experienced this pain firsthand with an ambitious start-up I was involved with called Outbox Mail. Outbox Mail sought to transform postal mail delivery by turning physical mail into a digital format for online viewing. Their method, however, ran into regulatory hurdles, especially from the US Postal Service (USPS). The USPS raised the issue of intercepting mail before it reached the recipient and handling someone else's mail, which might breach tampering laws, even with user permission. But the real objection was that Outbox aimed to help users opt out of junk mail. Outbox thought the USPS would think this was a great feature since customers loved it, but they learned a hard and counterintuitive lesson. The USPS derives significant revenue from junk mail by ensuring advertisers that their mail will reach households no matter what. Rather than recognizing Outbox as a potential partner, USPS saw it as a direct threat to this crucial income source. The postal service's refusal to cooperate rendered Outbox's business model unviable, leading to its closure.

But ultimately, the biggest failure mode I see with insights is the same as the most common failure mode with inflections: a lack of specificity. This is where the stress test can be valuable.

A stress test allows you to get specific about:

- the insight
- the different future it makes possible
- the inflections that enable it
- the reason it's non-consensus
- the reason it's right
- the reason the timing is right

INSIGHT TAKEAWAYS

1. Breakthrough start-up ideas need a fundamental insight, which requires you to be non-consensus and right. It's not enough to build a better mousetrap because lots of other start-ups and incumbents are likely doing so already, and that will cause your upside opportunity to be competed away. The path to greatness is to be both non-consensus and right about an opportunity to change how people will think, feel, and act in the future.

2. Powerful insights leverage the power of inflections. You don't want to be contrarian for its own sake. Your insight needs to be based on inflections rather than on a clever tagline. You could mistake "Betcha can't eat just one" for an insight that worked for Lay's potato chips, but it is not based on powerful inflections. Discovering a meaningful insight is not only about being clever; the insight that drives a breakthrough needs to have substance. It needs to leverage the power of inflections, the underlying mechanisms that give an insight the momentum to create radical change.

3. Powerful insights contradict conventional wisdom, which means many people will disagree with yours. Things we take for granted today were once considered heresy in their time. When Galileo endorsed Copernicus's insight that planets revolve around the sun in a heliocentric model, thus challenging the accepted belief that they revolved around the earth in a geocentric model, he was put on trial by the Roman Catholic church in 1633. He was found "vehemently suspect of heresy" and was forced to recant his views. He spent the rest of his life under house arrest. It wasn't until 1822, almost two centuries later, that the Catholic church formally lifted its ban on books promoting heliocentrism. Ignaz Semmelweis proposed that handwashing could drastically reduce the incidence of fever and death in hospitals. He was met with skepticism and ridicule by the medical community. While he wasn't threatened with violence directly, his life ended tragically in a mental institution. Charles Darwin hesitated to publish his theory of natural selection. He recognized the religious implications and how his ideas challenged prevailing beliefs about creation. He feared backlash from religious circles. Professionally and socially, he was concerned about the reactions of peers, friends, and family. His discovery that Alfred Russel Wallace had similar ideas spurred him to publish, and in 1859 Darwin's *On the Origin of Species* was released. Not surprisingly, it ignited significant debate and controversy on the way to laying the foundation for modern evolutionary biology.

4. So much around us that we accept as given today came from insights that were considered heresy in their time. But it turns out that, regardless of your field, to achieve a massive breakthrough you must be willing to depart from conventional wisdom. This is counterintuitive behavior; it goes against what we learn growing up. We are rewarded with better grades when we give known answers to questions that have already been discovered. We get rewarded with better health if we work out more hours in the gym. Most things we do are rewarded when we produce more of something. But breakthroughs are different from conventional or incremental success. They require you to think and act differently. In the chapters ahead, you'll discover how founders we've already introduced, including Justin Kan and Emmett Shear of Twitch, Osman Rashid and Aayush Phumbhra of Chegg, and Logan Green and John Zimmer of Lyft, bravely upheld their groundbreaking visions. Each faced challenges, skepticism, and the pressure to conform.

5. It takes courage to pursue an insight. When you set out to build a start-up based on what you think is a breakthrough idea, you won't know for certain, even after stress-testing it, if you are right, and perhaps not even whether you are non-consensus. But you must depart from the consensus if you want to pursue an idea that has the upside potential that will reward your sacrifice. Consensus ideas and breakthrough results have an inverse relationship. The more consensus your idea is, the more likely people are to agree with it already, which

means the more likely it is to have competition, even if you do not yet know who the competition is. Conversely, the best insights often result in monopolies: because they defy conventional wisdom, no one else is pursuing them at first.

6. Stress-test your insights by considering them in sufficient detail. Rather than just proposing something contrarian for its own sake, ask: What is going to be different in a nonobvious way? Which specific inflections will make this possible for the first time? What does the consensus think, and how am I different? Why am I right? What do I know about the future that the consensus doesn't know? Why is the imminent future the right time for my insight to hold true? Why hasn't it already happened?

Discovering compelling insights is where the true artistry of breakthrough founders lies. It takes creativity to understand the implications of new technologies and see novel ways of connecting them to bring about radical change.

Making a case, as we have, for discovering meaningful insights raises additional questions. Where is the best place to look for them? How do you determine whether you are on to something or not? Those answers come next.

6

LIVING IN THE FUTURE

Where You Will Find Your Next Insight

The future is already here; it's just not evenly distributed.
—WILLIAM GIBSON, AUTHOR,
COINED THE TERM "CYBERPUNK"

Marc Andreessen was a student at the University of Illinois in the winter of 1992, earning minimum wage as a programmer at the school's National Center for Supercomputing Applications (NCSA). Despite his meager earnings, he found more important riches in the next-generation technology that surrounded him. NCSA was a hub for supercomputing and high-speed networking, bolstered by generous funding from the government's National Science Foundation. NCSA stood as a crucial node in a network of minds and machines igniting the early wildfire called the internet.

Andreessen and his colleague Eric Bina were living at technology's front lines, tinkering at its boundaries. At the same time, the US government was starting to open the internet for commercial use. Tim Berners-Lee had invented the World Wide Web and recently turned it loose in the public domain.

Marc and Eric were living in the future.

Despite the fact that they had access to technology most could only dream about, the software that could unlock its potential was primitive at best. Seeing firsthand what was lacking, Marc and Eric set out to build the software they thought should exist.

People who ran things in the big institutions of the present could be forgiven for not noticing. They were engrossed in a question that mattered to them far more: Who would build what they called the digital superhighway?

Some thought telecommunications and cable companies would lead due to their widespread physical networks. They would expand their current telephone lines or cables and provide the new "pipes" to meet emerging digital needs. Others believed that tech companies like Microsoft or AOL would be front-runners. Microsoft was building the Microsoft Network (MSN) and echoed AOL's approach of a "walled garden." They aimed to create, curate, and control the content flowing through their networks. Their consumer software and PC market dominance cast them as strong contenders.

Some thought that perhaps the government should take it on. After all, DARPA's vision, funding, and research had already laid the foundational technologies and protocols that would beget the internet.* One could draw an analogy to how, in the second half of

---

* DARPA is the Defense Advanced Research Projects Agency, the research and development arm of the US Department of Defense.

the twentieth century, the government had successfully laid the concrete interstate highways that changed how Americans lived.

People expected the digital superhighway to be a top-down effort. Few imagined the alternative: a bottom-up approach, born in a different future.

Behind the scenes, several inflections were gathering that weren't apparent to most of the people living in the present. The first inflection, mentioned above, was the government's decision in 1991 to open the internet to commercial traffic. The number of access points and the connections among its users were increasing, and the pathways that carried digital traffic were increasing in capacity at an exponential rate. Recently crafted standards marked another inflection. These included the Uniform Resource Locator (URL), HyperText Transfer Protocol (HTTP), and HyperText Markup Language (HTML).

Nobody imagined that a college kid earning minimum wage in a computer lab would completely change the conversation—by developing the world's first user-friendly internet browser.

But Marc, Eric, and a few other colleagues did. Because they were living in the future, they were interacting on a daily basis with the new, enabling technologies of the internet and cultivating new ways of thinking, feeling, and acting through those interactions. The team realized that the winning metaphor wasn't a digital superhighway, with traffic speeding along a well-defined path, and fixed exit and entrance ramps controlled by the big players. The internet was instead like a web—something alive with unanticipated, multivariate, multidimensional dynamism; something organic, messy, hard to explain, and constantly extending itself. In fact, they didn't think in terms of whether they agreed or disagreed with the notion of a digital superhighway. They were thinking independently about the problems they faced. They weren't contrarian in the sense that they disagreed with the conventional wisdom. They were solving the problems they were independently interested in, from a wholly different perspective. Their different perspective led to Mosaic, the first user-friendly internet browser that would cross over into the mainstream. It would start a revolution.

SURFING THE WAVES OF THE FUTURE

Mosaic's story illustrates an important lesson about founders who create a breakthrough: they're almost always living in the future, immersed in the process of cultivating new patterns of thinking, feeling, and acting through ongoing interaction with new, empowering technologies and with other people who are also living in the future.

Most people have the wrong idea about how breakthrough ideas develop. They tend to think it's about having a "vision"—as if someone is seeing farther over the horizon than others through a better pair of binoculars. Or they are simply struck by an idea, the way Isaac Newton supposedly came up with the theory of gravity when he was hit on the head by a falling apple.

Most people think breakthrough insights come from having better ideas about the future. But the most effective approach I have seen to unearthing breakthrough insights comes from something more visceral. Breakthrough insights come from living in the future and tinkering directly with what's new about it—not by having passing ideas about it from a distant vantage point.

Why is this?

Remember how we earlier said that pattern-breaking ideas introduce something new that creates radical change in how people think, feel, and act? Living in the future is the way you escape the baked-in assumptions of the status quo. It's how you get directly acquainted with new assumptions that can lead to compelling insights.

You need to experience firsthand the new powers that inflections confer on people. By interacting with that thing—by using it, experimenting with it, probing its powers—and by interacting with other people who are also living in the future, you begin cultivating new patterns of behavior, different from those that characterize the status quo.

These new patterns enable you to break free from the constraints that shape the beliefs, desires, expectations, and ambitions of people living in the present. They enable you to see that the way people live at present isn't compulsory. The world as it exists now—the world that is—represents just one way among many that the world could be.

To further clarify this idea of living in the future, and why it's so vital, consider our next notable pattern breaker, Bob Metcalfe, the ethernet's coinventor. In the 1970s, Bob was at Xerox PARC (Palo Alto Research Center), which holds a unique place in the annals of computing history. Xerox PARC was the birthplace of game-changing technologies like the mouse, the windowing interface, and the laser printer, years before they were popularized by Apple and others. While there, Bob co-created the ethernet to enable all the people with these advanced Xerox computers to share a laser printer.

Bob likens his experience at Xerox PARC to living in a "time machine." Even though the computers at PARC were expensive, it was clear to him that someday everyone would have computers quite like what he was working with. In his efforts to network computers at the lab to share one of the world's first laser printers, he came to believe that his insights into interconnectivity would be valid someday for most computer users. This led him to start 3Com, one of the first major PC Ethernet companies. His insight was spot-on. Ethernet emerged as the leading networking standard due to its simplicity, adaptability, and versatility, seamlessly integrating local and wide area networks.

Marc Andreessen and Bob Metcalfe both tackled issues rooted in their advanced computing experiences, anticipating that their solutions would become essential for the broader public as technology evolved to match their current environment. Crucially, in both instances, Marc and Bob didn't need to discard old habits to develop innovative solutions. Instead, by immersing themselves in environments representing a future that only a few were witnessing, they gained fresh perspectives. This direct experience with new challenges naturally guided them to nonobvious insights.

Interestingly, the insights uncovered by Marc Andreessen and Bob Metcalfe that led to Netscape and 3Com show how living in the future can unearth ideas that morph into groundbreaking businesses without the initial intent of starting companies. Airbnb and Facebook are more recent examples. Airbnb, as we described earlier, began as a way for Brian Chesky and Joe Gebbia to get extra money for rent. They set up a WordPress site to rent out their apartment during a design conference. Mark Zuckerberg launched "thefacebook" as a college project aimed at connecting

Harvard students. Although these efforts started without corporate ambitions, both benefited from their founders' roots as digital natives. Millennials born between 1981 and 1996 had not typically led major companies yet. Many were still navigating their teenage years. Yet, Chesky and Zuckerberg, born in 1981 and 1984 respectively, were among the first of their generation to steer companies that would significantly shape the early twenty-first century.

When we described the inflections for Airbnb, we categorized Millennials as digital natives. For them, digital wasn't just an accessory; it was in the fabric of their everyday life experiences. The term "computer" for these folks didn't just represent some adjunct tool; it was where life pulsated. These people matured with the internet as their playground, smartphones as their trusted sidekicks, and social media as their town square. Zuckerberg and Chesky, standing at the forefront of this wave, weren't merely the latest up-and-coming tech leaders. They had a unique understanding of the preferences of digital natives, who were soon to become the most dynamic customers of emerging technology.

Another key difference had to do with how the technology they were interacting with was about to change how products could be built, not just how they were used. Before the year 2000, engineers at technology companies constantly looked for creative ways to work around constraints. Even though computers and networks kept improving, engineers faced limitations in processing power, memory, storage, and bandwidth. They had to creatively minimize negative experiences for customers in areas where the technology may have fallen short.

By 2004, when Mark Zuckerberg launched Facebook, the limits imposed by those constraints flipped into abundant growth drivers. Broadband became widespread, enabling online services to reach vast audiences. Open-source software, like the LAMP stack, provided free critical infrastructure. Start-ups no longer had to buy expensive and proprietary hardware, databases, and tooling. Soon, Amazon Web Services would eliminate the need for start-ups to maintain their own infrastructure; start-ups could run and update their products in the cloud, bypassing the traditional cumbersome process of upgrading individual company-managed servers. This enabled founders like Zuckerberg to continually refine products based on real-time feedback and aggressively run growth-oriented experiments. And it allowed Brian Chesky to lean into his penchant for design-driven thinking and the customer experience without needing to worry as much about the plumbing that supported it. In other words, both founders learned about how to build technology businesses at the precise time when the assumptions about how to build them were about to change. There was now a new pattern for how to think about and execute the task of building and distributing new products. There was nothing for Brian and Mark to unlearn—it was the first and only model they had known, a gift from the future.

The biggest challenge to creating a breakthrough start-up is overcoming the limitations imposed by the established patterns of thinking shared by people living in the present. These patterns prevent most people, including potential founders, from recognizing inflections and the potential for radically different futures. Living in the future enables you to emerge with insights—the second essential element of inflection theory—into how the new things you're interacting with can lead to a powerful and nonobvious insight that will make a significant difference for people in the future.

FINDING WHAT IS MISSING IN THE FUTURE

Marc Andreessen and Bob Metcalfe each found their way to a breakthrough insight by solving a problem for themselves. They created a solution to a challenge they were already experiencing while living in the future. There's a certain magic in crafting something with your own hands, for your own needs. As Paul Graham, the cofounder of Y Combinator, eloquently put it, "Why is it so important to work on a problem you have? Among other things, it ensures the problem really exists. It sounds obvious to say you should only work on problems that exist. And yet by far the most common mistake start-ups make is to solve problems no one has."

Why would so many people make such an obvious mistake? It's because we often fall in love with our idea of the solution we want to build before falling in love with a problem that we experience while living in the future. "Falling in love with a solution" highlights the danger that founders, creators, or teams can become so enamored with their particular product or service—their "solution"—that they overlook whether it actually solves a real problem for their customers.

This can lead to developing products that are technically impressive or aesthetically pleasing, but that don't resonate with users because they don't solve a significant problem or improve people's lives in a meaningful way.

Success comes from falling in love with the problem. By deeply understanding and caring about the problem, founders are more likely to build something people desperately want. Some problems deserve your love more than others. The best problems to chase are those that exist in the future. Pattern-breaking ideas are less about conjuring up the next big thing for tomorrow and more about genuinely understanding tomorrow's problems before others are exposed to them.

But what if you're not fortunate enough to be hanging out in a supercomputer lab or some other time machine at exactly the right moment? What if you don't yet have an insight that meets your own burning desire to solve your own problem?

The good news is that there's more than one way to live in the future and identify what's missing there. Consider Okta, which provides customers with unified access to all their cloud apps. CEO Todd McKinnon was head of engineering for Salesforce when he and his colleague Frederic (Freddy) Kerrest cofounded Okta, first called Saasure, in 2009. Todd's and Freddy's roles at Salesforce, just when the company was starting to take off, had put them on the front lines of the cloud-computing revolution. It gave them a major advantage in understanding the challenges experienced by the pioneering customers who first adopted cloud computing. Todd and Freddy enjoyed informal yet trusting relationships with those clients, and this allowed Todd and Freddy to get to the crux of the clients' most pressing issues. Both founders knew that the problems of their leading-edge customers were highly likely to be problems that lots of customers would face over time as cloud-based products became more mainstream.

Todd McKinnon's situation was different from the prior examples we've described in an important way: his team was solving a problem for customers they knew were living in the future.

Todd's vantage point as vice president of engineering at Salesforce, a trailblazing company in cloud computing, gave him a proprietary view of the future, even if not quite as directly as if he'd been solving his own personal problem. Before Salesforce's ascent, companies relied primarily on on-premises software, hosting their business software in-house on their own computers and data centers. Salesforce changed this by offering software that Salesforce managed on behalf of the customer in the cloud. Marc Benioff, Salesforce's founder, highlighted the cloud's benefits, like cost effectiveness, scalability, remote accessibility, and automated software updates.

While the early adoption phase had its skeptics, cloud computing's value proposition gradually gained mainstream acceptance. What set Todd and Freddy apart? Their hands-on experience with Salesforce's customers meant they knew the first true believers in cloud computing extremely well. Their experience at the leading edge revealed a new pattern: these clients were rapidly adopting other cloud services. And they were struggling with new issues as they expanded their use of cloud computing beyond Salesforce. As they deployed more and more cloud applications, they needed to create separate log-ins for each application their users wanted to access. They needed a solution that would allow each user to access all their cloud applications from one place with the same log-in.

Todd's vantage point allowed him to foresee the day when business clients wouldn't be using only Salesforce or Workday, but hundreds of cloud-based applications, each with a different password. Managing that would be a colossal pain. He could envision a day when lots of customers implemented a multitude of cloud offerings, not just the early believers he had interacted with.

Further, he saw that the challenge was already impacting those at the cutting edge of cloud adoption, and that the tools of the present wouldn't suffice to address it.

If anybody could build a unified access management tool for early adopters of the cloud, it would be Todd and Freddy. Not only did they know the early customers and their pains, but the customers trusted them as fellow co-conspirators. They were members of the same tribe; the customers knew Todd and Freddy, and they knew their work at Salesforce and what they were building at Okta. Today, Okta has more than six thousand corporate customers, with hundreds of millions of users on its platform.

Okta is one example of a company that serves customers who live in the future. There are others, especially companies who intend to serve business customers. But what if you aren't living in the future by solving a problem for yourself, the way Marc was, or living in the future by solving a problem for others whose problems you know firsthand, the way Todd did?

Can you transport yourself to the future? It turns out the answer is yes.

7

GET OUT OF THE PRESENT

Avoiding a Common Entrepreneur Mistake

Live in the future, then build what's missing.
—Paul Graham, cofounder, Y Combinator

M addie Hall is the CEO and cofounder of Living Carbon, a biotech start-up that uses genetic engineering to create "supertrees" that grow faster and capture and store more carbon from the atmosphere than normal trees. She took another path to live in the future.

Maddie was employed as a product manager at a Silicon Valley company called Zenefits, a cloud-based human resources platform. She decided she wanted to start a new company and initially went about it by trying to think of start-up ideas. But then she made a very wise decision: she decided to work on special projects with Sam Altman instead. Sam was one of the first entrepreneurs to go through Y Combinator, and he later served as YC's president for several years. Now Sam leads OpenAI, a pioneering force in AI research, aiming to make artificial general intelligence (AGI) a universally beneficial tool. Maddie took a job with OpenAI for a different reason than the immediate potential upside of the stock or how she might be compensated. Her tour of duty with Sam offered her two pivotal opportunities.

First, being at OpenAI gave Maddie an unparalleled vantage point into the evolving AI landscape. She witnessed firsthand the creation of innovative models like GPT-3 and DALL·E. OpenAI's dedication to releasing open-source AI tools, paired with a stellar team of AI experts, placed Maddie right at the nexus of AI advancements. Its strong focus on safety and its dedication to responsibly deploying AGI meant that OpenAI would also play a significant role in AI ethics and policy dialogues across multiple sectors, from art to law to medicine. Maddie had the opportunity to immerse herself in these important discussions. OpenAI was poised to foster an alumni network full of influential individuals whom it would be beneficial to know in numerous future scenarios.

Second, shadowing Sam offered Maddie an invaluable learning experience. Altman's forward-thinking approach and interactions with some of the tech world's brightest minds gave Maddie diverse perspectives on the future. Her position enabled her to understand various potential technological trajectories through OpenAI's initiatives and Sam's engagement with companies that were also on the leading edge of commercializing AI. This was, undeniably, a unique chance to witness multiple facets of the future concurrently. She also gained insights from numerous business leaders and policymakers beyond the tech sector that Sam engaged with.

It's hard to imagine a better-crafted opportunity to glimpse not only one but multiple futures. Following Sam around gave Maddie a front-row seat to the future. She spent day after day meeting brilliant and ambitious people, all pursuing their own futures.

Maddie is passionate about climate change, and the roots (pun intended) of the future she inhabited lay in her past. Her grandmother was a botanist. Her father is an entrepreneur. Her uncle has a logging company. One day during a meeting at Microsoft, she listened as executives described how they were energized about doing something real to address carbon in the atmosphere. She noted their significant commitment to addressing climate change. They vowed to become carbon negative by 2030 and to erase their entire carbon history by 2050. Microsoft set up a $1 billion Climate Innovation Fund to advance carbon reduction technologies. The executives promised transparency with comprehensive carbon reporting and aimed to implement an internal carbon tax. Additionally, Microsoft was focused on ensuring the carbon neutrality of companies in its supply chain and was developing a sustainability calculator for cloud customers to assess and diminish their carbon impact. As Maddie's travels with Sam continued, she noticed more executives at other large corporations starting to talk in the same way. She also observed that while policymakers and businesses were doing fantastic work on the issue, not many radical new technologies were being brought to market that could address it. One path stood out for her: plant biotechnology. She noticed something else too: a number of brilliant tenured researchers in academia who planned to go into biotech because they had devoted their lives to working on plants.

The possibilities intrigued her. She wondered if her passion for start-ups could provide the spark to animate some of these people in academia to start a business with her—but first she realized she needed to learn more. To live in that future. She became obsessed with understanding the research projects that could bring new technologies to bear in addressing climate change through genetically modified trees. And that led her to botanist and paleobiologist Patrick Mellor, who became her cofounder and chief technology officer.

Maddie's unique position in the future made her among the first to see the opportunities. She and Patrick set up a company that supports both lab and field research and implementation on multiple species of trees. This in turn made it easier for them to attract some of the most talented scientific and technical minds in the field.

Maddie had recognized two powerful inflections: first, the recent research that made it possible to introduce technology to genetically modify trees to grow faster and take more carbon from the atmosphere; and second, a tipping point in corporate America's willingness to allocate part of their budget to addressing climate change. Living Carbon harnesses the power of these inflections to radically change how people go about removing carbon from the atmosphere and the rate at which they do so.

FIND WHAT IS MISSING

Maddie didn't develop her start-up idea in a conventional way. She didn't conduct a top-down market assessment, looking for customer pain points and gaps in the markets, or by coming up with ideas for a start-up by interviewing a bunch of customers about their needs.

Direct engagement with customers and careful market assessment are key contributors to success. But Maddie understood another crucial factor to consider. She decided to get out of the present. Spending time with Sam Altman was her vehicle. It eventually carried her to a future that was authentically hers. The bet she placed on that future became the insight that led to Living Carbon. Most people live in the present, but not everyone. Yes, it is possible to come up with a breakthrough insight by living in the present, but the odds are dramatically worse. If you're like most founders we work with, you'd rather improve your odds wherever possible!

The idea of living in the future as opposed to living in the present strikes some as a semantic difference rather than a concrete notion. Isn't the very act of creating any start-up an effort to live in the future, by definition? Aren't start-up founders envisioning a different tomorrow? You might be inclined to agree, and I can see where you are coming from. But hear me out for a bit because there's an important nuance that's easy to miss. Let's take a closer look at the difference between living in the present and living in the future.

Deciding where you "live" is a choice that most founders don't even realize they are making. Should I build my start-up based on the assumption that the future will be a continuation of the present, following similar patterns and rules? Or do I build for a future that I believe will be radically discontinuous, where the norms and assumptions of today shift dramatically?

When founders build for a future that's an extension of today, they are living in the present, building on present-day norms of thinking, feeling, and acting that have been previously set by others. They focus on creating a better future—an improved version of the present. Living in the present is enticing because the route to success is more straightforward and recognizable. Your cofounders, investors, and advisors will be less likely to push back on your ideas. But in this clarity and comfort lies a trap, because following existing rules inherently constrains your potential to achieve outsized impact.

The pattern breaker seeks to build for a future that will break from what we know today. They are living in the future. They reject the path of refining what already exists. They focus on creating a radically different future and commit to discovering inflections and insights that enable them to deliver a pattern-breaking solution. Living in the future is not for everyone; very few have the inner confidence to take that path. You're piecing together a path forward without a clear map to guide you. However, it's precisely this absence of preset landmarks and limits that offers enormous potential. You're not confined by the boundaries established by others; instead, you have the freedom to create new boundaries.

Whether one lives in the present or the future starts with having the right mindset, but it also comes from hands-on work with technology inflections that can create the necessary shifts. Immersion in technology inflections—while also teaming up with the right collaborators, who have their eyes on the same point on the horizon—amplifies your abilities to see the new patterns of thinking, feeling, and acting that will come with the changes ahead.

As described earlier, at the start of commercial use of the internet, people living in the present believed that the digital superhighway would be built and defined by the old guard—the

phone and cable companies, the tech giants, or the state. People
from that world believed that the world of tomorrow would extend
out from current patterns. For instance, Microsoft believed they
had to construct a superior walled garden, one that outdid AOL's,
and link it closely with their Windows operating system. Microsoft management took their cues by listening to the needs of Windows users, and why not? These were the people whose problems
Microsoft cared the most to solve.

The Mosaic team, by contrast, was living in the future, developing software on advanced hardware with powerful computing
and graphics capabilities, and making use of the newly released
protocols of the World Wide Web. Very few people had been
exposed to such advanced capabilities. Even fewer were able to
build something new based on those capabilities. The Mosaic
team decided what to build by directly observing the obstacles
they faced while trying to unlock the full potential of the new
capabilities. They were getting feedback from like-minded early
internet users, who were also living in the future and exploring
this uncharted territory. The team created a solution that was radically different from the walled gardens favored by those living in
the present; they decided that their approach should not be constrained by top-down thinking—it should be more like a web.

The difference can be simply described by looking at the starting point. If you are living in the present, your starting point is the
present and you extrapolate into the future. If your starting point
is living in the future, you can't extrapolate from the present.
People living in the future have a better vantage point to develop
an insight earlier; those in the present will be playing catch-up.
People living in the present build solutions for problems in the

present. That may result in a successful company, but it is only an extension of the present and likely to offer only incremental change to the status quo.

Living in the future is easier said than done. But Peter and I believe it is the most effective method for arriving at insights that can achieve the highest impact.

It's very difficult to recognize whether something has the potential to radically change how people live. The best way to grasp how something empowers people is to experience its empowering potential for yourself. Most people can't see the potential of a new technology because they're limited by their preexisting ideas of how things work. Their established patterns of life limit their imaginations. They're too stuck in the mode of thinking about how things are to understand how things could be. Ironically, most people's limiting beliefs are self-imposed. They block themselves from having insights about the future.

Pattern-breaking founders, by contrast, break free of conventional ways. They're able to see things that most people can't—a world without the limitations of the present. Their liberation enables them to grasp the potential for change that a new technology introduces. That's what enables them to gain an insight about how things could be.

By living in the present you might have a vague general sense that there must be inflections all around. But you wouldn't know exactly where they are and what the empowering technologies are. By living in the future, though, you learn specifically where there's an inflection and what the new, empowering technology is. You're exposed to the inflection before other people—and you have a much more visceral experience of the new technology and the capacities it confers on people. You are then able to explore the limits of the new capabilities and gain a far more practical and authentic understanding of the ways the technology can truly help people, and where it's still too limited to be useful.

Living in the future also enables you to notice what's missing in the future. While you interact with other people living in the future and tinker with the new powers that emerging technologies confer, you encounter obstacles to making the new technology do the things you want. You think, "If only I had something that would overcome this obstacle." What you wish for is what's missing from the future that you inhabit. The Mosaic team was looking to solve problems in the future they inhabited—which led to innovations that would make the internet more useful to them, to the people they worked with, and, as it turned out, to the rest of humanity.

A select group of founders are living in the future. They might be the only people who have ever encountered an obstacle there. As a result, there are often no preexisting solutions they can avail themselves of. They must come up with novel solutions on their own, just as Marc Andreessen and the Mosaic team did.

By getting familiar with the unfamiliar, you become enabled to see the transformative potential that everyone else misses—the pockets of the future distributed unevenly among us. You see that the world that now exists isn't the world that needs to be. Not only is there a world that could be; there is a world that should be.

Many venture capitalists talk about their desire to invest in domain experts. To be more precise, what you really want to be is a domain expert about a meaningful future. And this happens when you go deep down the rabbit hole of experiencing the future and interacting with the things and people who are there.

Since few people choose to live in the future, few perceive opportunities on the horizon to change the rules with new technology. Your future-oriented vantage point provides you with the dual advantages of clearer perceptions and minimal distractions. The clarity comes from the freedom to immerse yourself in exploring emerging technologies, shaping your distinct viewpoints from firsthand experiences. Additionally, being surrounded by others who share this forward-looking perspective amplifies the quality of your learnings as they, too, engage with the new realities alongside you. This not only bolsters your understanding but also shields you from the prevalent skepticism of the present-minded majority, who often dismiss new tech and ideas as irrelevant or doomed to fail. This sharpening of your observational skills allows you to discover fundamental insights long before they become apparent to others.

You can also live in the future by spending time with certain types of people on the internet, on platforms like Reddit. Patrick Collison, Stripe's cofounder and CEO, suggests, "Make friends over the internet with people who are great at things you're interested in. The internet is one of the biggest advantages you have over prior generations. Leverage it."

Reddit is a haven for many entrepreneurs exploring future-focused start-up ideas. With its diverse "subreddits" that cater to various interests, from technology to sustainability, it fosters active, in-depth discussions. Redditors, often early adopters and tech aficionados, freely share insights, aided by the platform's relative anonymity. This global community offers a mix of collaborative brainstorming, real-world feedback, and a pulse on emerging trends. Moreover, networking opportunities abound, with tales of start-up successes and missteps providing invaluable lessons. For visionaries, Reddit is an ideal testing ground for innovative concepts. X/Twitter is also an energetic hub for future-focused entrepreneurial inspiration and collaboration. With access to diverse experts and real-time trends, users can engage in deep conversations that offer unique perspectives, and they can forge new relationships with people across the world. Direct interactions with industry leaders, curated content lists, and immediate feedback loops can help you generate and refine your ideas in areas that interest you most. Other future-dwellers have encountered fellow time travelers and potential co-conspirators while exploring online forums like Hacker News and Product Hunt.

What are the characteristics of people who did not hesitate to break the pattern of the present? They have unconventional ways of thinking, feeling, and acting—behaviors that will familiarize you and get you comfortable with that different future. Sam Altman is a good example. Like Sam, these are people who favor change for the sake of an aesthetically better future, people who are passionate, motivated, and even driven by the idea of initiating that change. They often aren't as transactional as most businesspeople, and their primary motivation is not where the biggest profits will come from or how to make the most money off the new trend.

They're more interested in the ideas themselves. Why? The transactional is characteristic of the mundane present that these people have been trying to escape. The transactional kills the joy of exploring ideas. People like these are more interested in whether you can add to the ideas they care about.

These people are builders of and passionate enthusiasts about the future they spend time in. They are neither tourists nor spectators. They want to be engaged with the new technology. They want to live in the future that it makes possible now, and they don't simply want to witness it from a distance and exploit its financial potential when the path later becomes clear.

Technology brings out both the dreamers and the greedy. Certain futures attract those looking to get rich quick more than other futures. The cryptocurrency sector has become center stage for this problem, drawing in too many people who are looking not to build but to cash in. Initial coin offerings (ICOs) have allowed founders to generate wealth without necessarily delivering on the impactful innovations they promised, often leaving the less savvy investor holding the bag. The sector has been rife with pump-and-dump artists, untrustworthy exchanges, and all manner of hucksters, including celebrities. I remain optimistic about the potential of cryptocurrency and crypto networks. But I am closely watching to distinguish between those driven by building for the future and those chasing fast money.

PREPARING YOUR MIND

Louis Pasteur famously said that "chance favors the prepared mind." Pasteur made significant contributions to the fields of chemistry and microbiology, including the development of vaccines and the discovery of the principles of microbial fermentation and pasteurization. His work often required meticulous preparation, observation, and interpretation, and he was known for his diligent and thoughtful approach.

The quote reflects Pasteur's belief that scientific discoveries often come from unexpected observations or accidents, but that the ability to recognize and understand those unexpected findings relies heavily on having a well-prepared and educated mind. The chance event itself isn't enough to lead to a breakthrough; it takes a trained mind to recognize the importance of what has been observed and to know how to apply it.

For Pasteur, this meant having a strong foundation in scientific principles, preparing experiments carefully, and utilizing an inquisitive and open-minded approach that was ready to be influenced by unexpected results. His sentiment can be applied to many fields beyond science, from business to the arts, where a well-prepared mind is more likely to recognize and take advantage of opportunities that might otherwise go unnoticed.

Having a prepared mind for a chance event can seem counterintuitive and even unsettling, because the path can be indirect and the next step is not obvious. People who try to plot a direct path to start-up success treat the task on par with answering questions in school. They engage in familiar patterns of thinking about a problem—and as a result they come up with familiar-sounding ideas that reflect the consensus.

Living in the future involves embracing the uncertainty of the future and spending time with specific types of technology as well as specific types of people. What you choose to work on and who you spend your time with defines you in many ways. This may come at a cost. You might have to forfeit a bigger paycheck or bragging rights with your more conventional friends and business acquaintances in exchange for spending time with people who live in the future and interact with new technologies.

LIVING IN THE FUTURE TAKEAWAYS

1. Don't think of a start-up. When you think of a start-up, you can get trapped by the limitations imposed by the established patterns of thinking shared by people living in the present. These patterns can prevent you from interacting with the powerful possibilities that inflections introduce. Interacting with possibilities is what leads you to the insights that beget breakthrough ideas, and it's those insights that have the power to create radically different futures. Your advisers—and your own instincts—may suggest that going straight to thinking of a start-up is the shortest path to a breakthrough. We see it differently. The best path to breakthrough start-up insights is to live in the future and notice what is missing there.

2. Living in the future is the best way to stack the deck in your favor to achieve a breakthrough idea. You live in the future by directly interacting with the cutting edge of new technologies and by thinking about how to unlock their potential to create radically different futures. As you live in the future, you will encounter barriers to getting the most out of the technologies you interact with, which will inform your intuition about the most important things missing. This intuition is far more likely to be right in guiding you to a powerful non-consensus insight.

3. There are lots of ways to live in the future. Be creative about how to get there. Many paths exist. Not being intentional about living in the future is a huge missed opportunity.

4. You can act in ways that increase your chances of finding
    a breakthrough insight. You can fine-tune your powers
    of observation by paying closer attention to the world
    around you and looking for patterns or connections that
    most people would not bother to consider. You can con-
    sistently and regularly read about a wide range of topics,
    learn new skills, and gather information from various
    sources to help stimulate creative thinking. Through play
    and experimentation, you can learn in great depth about
    new ideas, materials, and techniques that can lead you to
    a breakthrough discovery. And you can pay careful atten-
    tion to your emotional and personal experiences, reflect-
    ing on your own feelings to generate inspiration.

Living in the future helps prepare your mind. And a prepared mind is much more likely to notice inflections and develop
insights about the profound changes they make possible. That's
why living in the future increases your chances of breaking out
of the consensus trap. Ultimately, though, you must be both
non-consensus and right. How can you ever be sure? That's the
topic we will turn to next.

Part II

Pattern-Breaking Actions

Unconventional Tactics to Make Breakthroughs Real

8

BEFORE YOU CROSS
THE RUBICON

The Implementation Stress Test

We are trying to prove ourselves wrong as quickly as possible, because only in that way can we find progress.
—RICHARD FEYNMAN, THEORETICAL PHYSICIST

L et's recap our journey so far. Breakthrough ideas come from authentically living in the future and understanding it far better than most, noticing powerful inflections you encounter there, and discovering a nonobvious insight that can lead to a radical change in how people will someday think, feel, and act. Some start-up founders are extremely talented, but not all opportunities are created equal. Profound insights, driven by significant inflections with the potential to shape the future, are the initial seeds of greatness.

When you have a start-up idea that excites you, it's tempting to go straight to developing a minimum viable product. But if you do so without first stress-testing whether your ideas embody powerful inflections and a compelling insight about the future, you reduce the chance of breakout success—even if you execute perfectly. Without the underlying powers required to create radical change and escape from competition, you risk pursuing incremental ideas with limited upside. This approach can result in reaching what mathematicians call a "local maximum."

You can visualize the idea of a local maximum. Imagine you're hiking and determined to climb the highest mountain in the area. You observe the highest peak, assess the route to the top, prepare your climb, and, after much effort, hopefully reach the summit. From the summit, you can now look farther into the distance, and you realize there are taller peaks out there. The peak you've just summited is the highest mountain locally, but that's because you started with a limited horizon and limited beliefs about what was possible for you to pursue. You would like to hike to one of the bigger peaks that you can see in the distance, but now you're stuck.

Navigating to higher peaks beyond the immediately obvious ones can be daunting, especially when they aren't clearly visible or you don't know with certainty that they exist. But it's possible to get beyond the local maximum with the right mindset, tools, and actions. By stress-testing your inflections and insights and ensuring that your insights are future oriented, you significantly increase your odds for a breakthrough.

The inflections stress test, introduced in Chapter 2, focuses on externalities. It is a sanity check to see if you are working on something that harnesses a massive change event. All things being equal, it's better to identify the most powerful inflections you can. It's also good if you can identify multiple inflections that might reinforce each other with their powers.

The insight stress test, introduced in Chapter 5, focuses on whether you have discovered something truly novel and surprising. It is a sanity check to see if you are non-consensus and right in leveraging powerful inflections that can lead to a potential breakthrough.

Inflections and insights, when effectively utilized, have their own individual potency, and they will amplify each other's impact. Strong inflections make your idea powerful by empowering people in new ways that delight them. Fundamental insights make your idea unique, which helps you escape the trap of competition. An idea that empowers greatly and stands apart uniquely is the best starting point to create a pattern-breaking start-up.

Using stress tests to validate your inflections and insights gets your start-up on the runway—but we're not yet cleared for takeoff. We need an additional stress test: the implementation stress test.

You are on the right path when your idea embodies a powerful inflection and you have a unique insight. But to deliver a product that breaks patterns and changes how people will think, feel, and act in the future, you need to identify the specific people who desperately want you to implement a specific solution. The implementation stress test helps you by creating a prototype with simulated features tailored to resonate strongly with a select group of early adopters. Once the right people see the right implementation of your prototype, they will be desperate to use the real version.

IMPLEMENTATION PROTOTYPES

Implementation prototype: A focused deliverable that helps you engage potential early believers to identify:

- What is the most important benefit?
- Who are the most desperate customers?

Chegg's implementation prototype, named Textbookflix, directly illustrates the idea. In late 2007, Chegg was in trouble. Founders Osman Rashid and Aayush Phumbhra had built a classified ads site for college students and had seen encouraging success. But their remaining cash had dwindled to four months of operating funds. Then Facebook, the most important start-up of the early 2000s, dropped a bomb, announcing it was entering the college classifieds market. Facebook had swept through college campuses everywhere, with students flocking to it instantly. At one point in 2007, almost every college student had a Facebook account.

Chegg thought it had found a fairly safe niche: classified ads catering to college students' needs, from textbooks to furniture. Facebook seemed more interested in social utility capabilities like sharing photos, making friend connections, and finding ways for people to connect in what they called a "social graph" than in entering the market for e-commerce and auctions. Chegg's progress was consistent, and the future seemed promising. But its cash balance was low, and it would soon need to begin fundraising. That didn't seem like a huge problem, considering its success to date as a classifieds site and its revenue growth expectations.

When Facebook announced its expansion into college classifieds, Chegg faced a new reality. If Facebook succeeded in classifieds, Chegg's business would be overshadowed instantly. And if Facebook stumbled in its attempt, potential investors would certainly question Chegg's chances of success. After all, if Facebook could not make college classifieds successful with its massive reach, how could a tiny upstart like Chegg possibly pull it off? With the clock ticking on their cash reserves, Chegg's survival was threatened. Without a compelling new direction and strong signs of customer desire, they wouldn't be able to secure more funding in time.

In prior months, Chegg had brainstormed the idea of textbook rentals, a concept they called Bookflix. But they hadn't pursued it because they didn't want to lose focus on their classifieds business. Now things had changed. It was at this bleak moment that inspiration, born of desperation, struck. Chegg's cash balance would drop to zero in a matter of months. They needed to pull a rabbit out of the hat. Because they were almost out of money, Chegg didn't have the funds to create even a basic version of a textbook rental system. They didn't have any textbooks to rent out or warehouses to store them in, a way to track orders and returns, or even a payment system. Without the capital to produce a real product, they went all-in on an implementation prototype of the textbook rental concept. The goal? To show prospective investors that college students would desperately want to rent textbooks, if given the chance. If they could prove this, they might secure additional funding to deliver an actual product and become a real business.

The implementation prototype they devised was an online service called Textbookflix. As you can see from Figure 8.1, it combined the look and feel of Facebook circa 2007 with a play on the name Netflix.

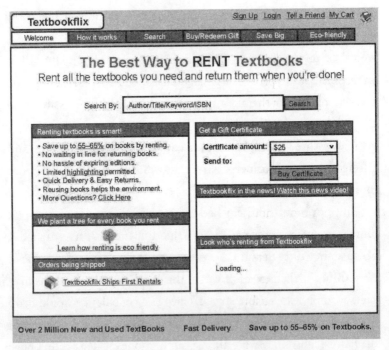

Figure 8.1 Textbookflix: Chegg's implementation prototype for textbook rentals.

Textbookflix appeared to offer the ability to rent textbooks. When students specified the books they wished to rent, the platform placed the books along with their rental prices in a shopping cart. At the end of the checkout process, the site appeared to crash, which meant the order couldn't be completed.

What was the point of launching a service that wasn't real? The founders of Chegg had calculated that if a new textbook was sold for $100, they needed to prove that a student would rent it for at least $35. And that belief could be tested on this concept site. Nobody knew that Textbookflix was from Chegg, so they could test something fake without damaging their reputation with future customers.

Textbookflix offered its "customers" textbook rental prices that were a random number between $35 and $75. This feature was another stroke of genius. It's tempting for founders to think of just needing to prove that their prices can exceed the minimum price required for the business to be viable, in this case $35. But Osman and Aayush pushed the envelope of what people would pay. Why stop at $35 or even $50? Why not see how much money they could get for each rental?

Which leads to another important point: a good implementation prototype should create results that surprise you, not just confirm your hopes or opinions. (More on this in the next chapter.) Chegg's founders did this not by asking, "Will students pay enough to cover our costs?" but by asking the better question: "How far can we push the price, and how can we determine the optimal price?" It turned out that many students were prepared to rent a $100 new textbook for upwards of $75. Students had no need for the textbook when they completed their course, so renting versus buying made perfect sense. College textbooks were expensive. A 25 percent savings was meaningful to many students.

Consider what Chegg learned from the Textbookflix implementation prototype. They could show prospective investors the willingness of college students to pay different rental prices in the real world. When you looked at the price students were willing to pay to rent textbooks on such a terribly presented site, it was obvious that there would be extraordinary demand for such a service.

Given the enthusiastic response from the implementation prototype, the founders were able to convince investors to provide the money they needed to deliver a real product as soon as possible. The Chegg team immediately shifted gears and started to build their minimum viable product with extraordinary urgency. It was an immediate hit with students, and the company's growth was nothing short of meteoric. In just five short years after testing the Textbookflix prototype, Chegg was moving an astonishing $200 million in textbooks. That was in 2012. Chegg then cemented its reputation with an initial public offering in 2013.

THE IMPLEMENTATION PROTOTYPE IS NOT THE MVP

People sometimes confuse an implementation prototype with a minimum viable product (MVP), but the two are different. An MVP is the most stripped-down version of a product that can still be released and used by early adopters. An implementation prototype is a step before creating your product. It seeks to validate whether your idea can become a product that specific customers will be desperate for once they fully grasp and connect with your concept.

An implementation prototype is like the concept cars displayed at auto shows. While these cars might look showroom ready at first glance, they aren't functional MVPs. For instance, the engine isn't operational, ignition buttons are nonresponsive, and dashboard gauges are static. Functions like the radio or air conditioning are merely for show. These concept cars aren't built for the road or safety tested.

Rather than presenting a production-ready car for early customers, automakers have a different objective with concept cars. They gauge audience interest and excitement for new ideas. The key question is: Do viewers eagerly want the concept car to become a reality, or do they simply pass by, drawn to something else? When creating and testing an implementation prototype, it's important to tailor the approach based on the product and the target customers. For online services or products, such as e-courses or subscription platforms, using landing pages might be an efficient way to test demand. These pages allow for quick feedback.

But quite often, something this basic isn't enough. Physical items, especially those reliant on sensory experiences like touch or taste, resist such a virtual test. When users face significant time or financial commitments, a webpage usually won't capture their interest with enough fidelity. Car manufacturers create concept cars to genuinely understand the reaction from car buyers and dealers. It's not just about viewing a car or hearing about it; it's about experiencing it. Making prototypes of cars that look real is costly, but it's essential for automakers to tease out whether customers are truly desperate for them to build the car.

Pattern-breaking founders master this balance. The goal when crafting an implementation prototype is to strike a balance between the effort put into the simulation and the kind of concrete feedback needed to gauge if your idea resonates strongly with potential early believers. Take Lyft as an example. Simple online ads or landing pages weren't enough to gauge rider and driver reactions. But founders Logan Green and John Zimmer wanted to know if people would be at ease sharing rides with strangers before releasing a product. They made a basic implementation prototype to bridge the gap. Initially, the founders and their friends drove, seeking firsthand feedback. Their cars wore giant pink mustaches, making them distinct and welcoming. To simulate rider demand before launching the official ride service, they used gig-working platforms like TaskRabbit to pay riders to gather genuine responses, refining the app based on feedback. While testing their implementation prototype, Lyft's founders and their team directly experienced many early riders eagerly telling them, "You have to build this app." It wasn't just the words; it was the fervor behind them. The founders weren't merely collecting feedback; they were witnessing a level of excitement and demand that seemed to be leading to something explosive.

As illustrated by these examples, this journey isn't guided by set formulas or a step-by-step playbook; it requires finesse, adaptability, and on-the-spot creativity. When considering the most effective implementation strategy, it helps to have a Guiding Question, a kind of North Star. Andy Rachleff, whom I referred to in Chapter 4, suggests one that I particularly like:

What can we uniquely offer that people are desperate for?

The word "desperate" can conjure an image of hopeless-ness or despair. Here, "desperate" implies a strong, positive craving—the kind of need that, once recognized, becomes an irre-sistible must-have.

Todd McKinnon and Freddy Kerrest also used the implemen-tation prototype approach when they developed the insight that led to Okta. Their experience in working with customers serves as an excellent illustration of adapting this focused-deliverable mindset to a business-to-business scenario.

Todd, when vice president of engineering at Salesforce, had a front-row seat to watch how the early adopters of cloud computing operated. He had a relationship with those customers and a reputation as someone who could do the job when it came to implementing business-critical solutions in the emerging cloud world.

Todd and Freddy, his cofounder and business partner, believed that early adopters of cloud computing were destined to struggle with managing and controlling their new cloud-centric environments in the same way that customers had struggled with managing other computing architectures before. As they tested their hypothesis about customers facing challenges in managing their growing collection of cloud applications, they weren't yet sure what customers would be desperate for.

Todd and Freddy began by designing mock-ups with a tool called Balsamiq. Their initial designs were very basic and highlighted the common technical issues they perceived companies would face with cloud applications. For instance, users might see error messages like "unable to connect" or "connection timed out." Or they might exceed resource limits in areas like storage or databases. They anticipated latency issues, representing delays rather than application failures, that would make applications seem slow. Todd and Freddy believed that a system to help businesses monitor and fix these issues would appeal to early adopters of cloud applications, so their mock-ups emphasized these capabilities.

The early mock-ups did not resonate with Okta's prospective customers the way Todd and Freddy had hoped. It wasn't that the issues they addressed were unheard of; rather, the vendors of the cloud world, like Salesforce, were already on it. Occasional hiccups like latency and connectivity? They were often managed and mitigated by the cloud providers themselves. The cloud, in essence, sold itself on handling these intricacies, and that was its allure. Many customers said something like, "That's interesting, but that issue is number four on my list of priorities." To which Todd and Freddy asked, "What's number one on your list?" Using the implementation prototypes as a catalyst for discussion with Salesforce customers, Todd and Freddy discovered that identity management was by far the top issue.

Identity management helps ensure that a company's employees have the right access to the right cloud services. Companies wanted their salespeople to be able to access sales data in Salesforce, but not the financial projections in NetSuite. Conversely, finance staff needed the opposite access privileges. When a new employee joined a company, the IT department had to help them set up accounts on Google Apps, internal wikis and intranets, health care and benefits, and many other corporate apps. Employees also needed an ever-increasing number of passwords for the cloud services they used personally, such as Dropbox and their online banking and brokerage accounts. Keeping track of all these passwords, one at a time, was a hassle, and the number of services hosted in the cloud kept increasing, adding further to users' pain. And when employees left a company, the IT department wanted to make sure that people couldn't continue to access their company systems for sensitive information about their customers or operational forecasts. They sought a cloud identity-management system to streamline cloud service access, enabling easy setup for new employees with the ability to remove them quickly from those systems if they left the company.

Todd and Freddy offered a great response to what they first heard: "Can we catch up again next week?" After buying some time, they returned to demonstrate a new version of their implementation prototype showing the very capabilities customers were most desperate to see in identity management. Todd and Freddy had started with the right insight: as users adopted more cloud applications, managing them would become complex. But their initial implementation of the insight missed the customers' top concern because Todd and Freddy had focused on resolving technical issues with cloud services, like connectivity and latency issues or resource allocation problems. Then, when they presented potential customers with an implementation prototype solution to review, the lukewarm feedback they received showed them what was not the top priority. From there, they were able to identify the customers' most pressing pain point: identity management.

In the examples we've highlighted for Lyft, Textbookflix (Chegg), and Okta, the cost and time required to create implementation prototypes were trivial compared to delivering even the most basic product release or minimum viable product. The founders were able to build these prototypes before raising any significant money from investors. The information they received from prospective customers convinced the founders they were on the right path. The data also helped them raise money because it provided evidence that customers would be desperate for their product.

Once you decide to raise money and staff up to build an MVP, you usually end up "crossing the Rubicon," even if you are not fully aware of doing so at the time. The expression comes from Julius Caesar's bold move in 49 BC to lead his army across the Rubicon River, thereby sparking Rome's civil war. The act was irreversible, signifying a point of no return. Now we use the phrase to mean a choice you can't undo, a final commitment.

From what I've observed, once start-up founders raise money and set about building a minimum viable product, they mentally and emotionally reach a point of no return. It's not helpful for them to learn after the fact that the forces underlying their start-up idea are not powerful enough to realize a big-enough upside. They are already fully committed.

Many jump too quickly to raise funding before confirming the power of their insight and identifying an initial set of passionate early believers. Having obtained the money, they hire developers, rent their first office space, and start developing a minimum viable product. And why not, since this is the standard recipe? Only later do many of these founders come to the realization they are trapped. They now have employees who took huge risks and likely pay cuts to join the cause. They have investors with expectations. They might have early customers who believed in them, even if not as many as they would like. They have followed all the best practices around agile development, getting out of the building to talk to customers, and mapping their ideas against the state-of-the-art frameworks for pricing and business model design. They even defined their culture proactively. They embraced all the tenets of disciplined entrepreneurship. But, still, something's missing. They aren't getting the traction they expected.

Why? Because customers are interested in what they have built, but they are not desperate for it.

Suddenly you realize that your idea isn't big enough. You followed the best practices for good execution, yet you've encountered the pitfall mentioned earlier in this chapter: settling for a limited upside, the dreaded local maximum. Knowing what you now know, you wouldn't have pursued this idea. But you feel like you can't abandon your commitments to employees, customers, investors—or even to your internal sense of not quitting. You are stuck.

Only now do you realize the true way to fail in a start-up. It is not about failure—or success—as most people describe it. The only way to truly fail in a start-up is to lose your time, especially after the point when you know the start-up was never worthy of it. The only thing you can never get back is that time.

Implementation prototypes allow you to increase your conviction before crossing the Rubicon. You want to validate your inflections, insight, and implementation first. You are better off taking these steps before you set out to build a minimum viable product.

9

SAVORING SURPRISES

How Early Customers Will Lead You to the Hidden Gems

Surprise is the greatest gift which life can grant us.
—Boris Pasternak, Russian poet and novelist

A few years ago, I was on a panel with Scott Cook, the founder and original CEO of Intuit, and regarded by many as one of the best product minds in the technology industry. For decades, he has prioritized deep understanding of customer needs in product development. In the 1980s, he introduced the "follow-me-home" strategy, where Intuit staff would observe customers using their products at home or work. This hands-on method helped identify both negative issues and features that delighted customers, more so than the company had expected. Numerous other tech companies, inspired by Intuit's success, adopted many of their winning approaches. During the Q&A, Scott mentioned that whenever a team presented a new product idea along with their research about its viability, he would ask, "What was the biggest surprise you encountered?"

When I heard him say this, it connected a bunch of disparate dots in my mind, yielding a new level of understanding about the value of surprises for the start-up process.

Surprises are so important to understand because you are pursuing a non-consensus idea for a future that is mostly unknown or at least ambiguous. You want to create a breakthrough product that people haven't seen before, not just an incremental improvement. Scott's comment helped me see that breakthroughs are a discovery of something new by definition—and that means they must have an element of surprise when they are encountered.

IMPLEMENTATION PROTOTYPES: YOUR TOOL TO UNCOVER SURPRISES

Engaging potential early customers with an implementation prototype previews your insight about the future to those who you hope are most desperate to benefit from it. Your insight about the future is hopefully spot-on. If your interactions with potential early customers cause you to conclude that the insight is false, you are far better off moving on rather than raising money, hiring a team, and investing your time and energy in a venture that's likely doomed.

Even if your insight is accurate, you're navigating a highly unpredictable terrain when interacting with early customers. Pitching an early prototype to potential customers is akin to laying out a map of what you believe the future holds. Sometimes that map leads to a treasure; at other times you can get feedback that suggests you're lost or have deviated from the right path. However, if your compass—your insight—points true, you receive guidance as to the general direction you need to head. Since you are traveling through unexplored territory, you should expect course corrections along the way. That's why not only should you expect surprises; you should savor them.

In the Okta example, feedback on the initial implementation prototype was tepid—a negative surprise. But by staying open to unforeseen feedback, Todd and Freddy pinpointed where the actual desperation lay, and they leaned into it when they iterated.

Sometimes, as with Chegg and Textbookflix, you find that your customers value your idea more than you might have guessed—a positive surprise. Chegg hoped students might spend at least $35 to rent a textbook rather than buy a new one for $100. The willingness of some students to pay up to $75 to rent a $100 textbook was a surprise. Looking back, anything less than $100 was an expense reduction, and for cash-strapped college students, even a small amount of extra money mattered. Chegg's story shows it is important to keep your mind open to positive surprises from early customer interactions. It suggests that when you're creating prototypes, you should aim for something that draws out the feedback you might not expect. This means you're often better off testing along a range using open-ended questions like "How much will a student pay?" than looking for a yes-or-no answer to "Will they pay $35?"

Both cases illustrate the profound importance of savoring surprises.

The idea of savoring surprises might seem obvious. Yet time and again, I've seen founders struggle to do it. Rather than venturing into the unknown with an eye toward noticing the unexpected, they approach early customers with a confirmation bias, aiming to validate their established hypotheses. It's not enlightenment they're primarily after, but affirmation. They hope for that reassuring nod, the "I knew it!" moment when their beliefs are echoed back to them. Yet they overlook the fact that each interaction with an early customer isn't just feedback—it's a chance to uncover a nugget of unforeseen wisdom. When founders overemphasize validation, they unintentionally shut the door to the profound lessons these interactions can offer. The essence of an implementation prototype is its ability to act as a conduit for unexpected revelations, allowing founders to refine and improve their concept based on these surprising discoveries.

If your insight is correct, you should be able to find specific people who are desperate for you to build a product implementing that insight. But as you explore whether this is indeed the case, there are two important variables for you to consider:

- Is this the best way to implement my insight?
- Am I talking to the right people?

When you encounter a negative surprise, it might be because you are implementing your insight wrong. But it might also be because you are talking to the wrong people, those who won't care about your insight no matter what you implement.

Keep in mind, if your idea is non-consensus, it follows that most people will dislike it—even if you are right. In the early days, people thought eBay was a silly website good only for selling PEZ dispensers. Many people thought AirBed and Breakfast was a crazy idea. Who would want to stay in a stranger's house? Or in the case of Lyft, get in a stranger's car? Or believe in a company like SpaceX that would launch reusable rockets into outer space?

Most "normal" people dislike even the most powerful and correct insights about the future because a true insight forces people to change their point of view in a way that can make them uncomfortable. Human beings are conditioned to favor the familiar. Paradoxically, that means if most people like your insight, it's probably not an insight at all. It's probably too similar to what they already know and like, which makes it more consensus than non-consensus.

This is why it's important to keep asking, "Am I talking to the right people?" in addition to "Is my implementation off target?" whenever you get negative feedback on your prototype.

The Okta example from the previous chapter illustrates this well. In the first iteration of their Balsamiq prototype, the founders were talking to the right people (early adopters of cloud computing and Salesforce) but showing the wrong initial implementation of their insight. It didn't land. So they kept listening to the right people, who gave them feedback about what they should build to best implement their insight.

Positive surprises are even more valuable. When you encounter a positive surprise, the key is to deeply understand "what went right" and lean into it aggressively. Start-up founders sometimes assume they should address objections as they iterate in their prototypes, but the real goal is to identify positive surprises and double down on iterations that reinforce them. This is an important distinction. The reason positive surprises matter most is they reveal desperation, which opens the door to success. Negative surprises are useful in determining that you haven't unlocked desperation, but they should not be looked at as objections you need to overcome. Instead, they should push you to iterate to seek positive surprises by modifying your implementation, modifying your audience, or a combination of both. Positive surprises suggest that you are getting warmer in your understanding of these two variables, which is why you want to pursue them aggressively.

SURPRISES ARE MORE VALUABLE
THAN VALIDATION

Positive surprises are awesome. They show that your idea might be right and non-consensus. They open the path to greatness if you lean into them because they uncover and shine an ever-brighter light on the truly desperate people who tangibly connect to your insight.

Negative surprises are also valuable because they inform your understanding in one of three ways: your implementation is wrong; you are talking to the wrong people; or your fundamental insight was wrong in the first place. If your insight was wrong, you have saved yourself the heartache of years spent on an idea that wasn't destined for the greatness you hoped to achieve. If you believe your insight is still right, then you can iterate on the people or the specific implementation of your insight until you unlock desperation and find yourself encountering positive surprises.

The ability to notice—and savor—surprises is a key overlooked skill of the greatest founders. It allows you to narrow in on the types of capabilities that will lead to breakthroughs. This can be counterintuitive because what often happens when we experiment is an effort to validate a hypothesis. But if we seek only validation, we will only confirm what we know. We also want to seek new learning that takes advantage of our first-mover advantage into the future.

GOOD, BETTER, DESPERATE

Why is it vital to find people who are desperate? A powerful inflection enables you to deliver something radically different, something that confers new capabilities that seem magical. A powerful insight allows you and only you to deliver these magical capabilities in a specific way not yet discovered by others. If you meet both conditions, then the people who value your advantage should be desperate for you to implement what you show them—because you are offering them a uniquely dramatic improvement in something they care deeply about.

If people have a good enough alternative relative to what you propose, you won't be different enough. For a breakthrough, you want to address an intense yet unresolved problem or desire. You're not trying to replace anything. You want to show people something they can't unsee in an area they care about deeply.

You want an implementation that causes potential customers to exclaim, "Where have you been all my life?!" when they see what you're talking about. It won't be most people. But for those who value your advantage, there will be no alternative for them to get what you can offer. This is why they will be desperate and why you should seek the desperate.

There's another benefit to finding desperate people. If you solve their problem, they will spread the word about your unique advantages to their friends. People like to share their discoveries when they know their friends will also be blown away. Being the first to discover the next great thing gives them social status and closer connections to people they care about.

THE CURSE OF TOO MANY BENEFITS

Andy Rachleff, whom we mentioned earlier, introduced me to the counterintuitive idea that offering customers too many benefits is a problem. In essence, by promoting too many benefits you confuse potential customers and dilute the main value proposition. Instead of clarifying the best reason that an early customer should be desperate for the product, offering too many benefits makes the decision process harder and more complex for customers.

By spreading too thin over numerous benefits, you risk being forgettable or failing to effectively communicate any one compelling reason for early customers to engage. Trying to be too many things to too many people ends up being nothing to nobody. In the world of start-ups, where capturing attention and differentiating oneself is already challenging, falling into this curse can be particularly detrimental.

Well-funded start-ups are often more susceptible to making this mistake because they have the money to hedge their bets rather than focus on what matters most. In our chapter on inflections, we mentioned the peril of Quibi, which folded only six months after launching in 2020, despite raising $1.75 billion and having a dream team that included Jeffrey Katzenberg and Meg Whitman. Besides their failure to leverage inflections, as discussed earlier, their tale was further muddled by the peril of offering an overabundance of benefits without a single compelling benefit that grabbed people's attention in a unique way. Qui-bi's deep pockets and giant ambitions resulted in a multifaceted approach, reflecting an attempt to cater to a wide range of tastes and preferences. Quibi marketed itself in many ways—from a Net-flix rival to a YouTube replacement and even an Instagram alter-native. Quibi did not zero in on a singular key benefit; it spread its value proposition thin, and this lack of clarity confused poten-tial users. Quibi represented too many benefits to potential users as it struggled to establish a distinct identity or niche for itself, which contributed to its challenges in capturing a loyal audience base.

As you design your implementation prototype, make sure you are clear about the most important question you want to val-idate regarding a prospective customer's desperation. In the case of Chegg, the most important question was "What is the limit of someone's willingness to pay to rent a textbook?" In the case of Okta, it was "What is the most urgent management problem early-adopter cloud customers are trying to solve right now?"

TIMEBOXING

The more often you iterate your implementation prototype, the more you can learn. You're also less attached to being "right" about a given iteration. Let's revisit the earlier example of automo-bile manufacturers displaying concept cars at an auto show. A car company unveils two different concept cars: car A that has every-one talking, and car B that generates very little interest. Since each showpiece lacks essential (and expensive-to-produce) com-ponents like an engine or a powertrain, the company has learned much in a short period of time (as measured in automotive years) and at a lower cost.

Similarly, after Chegg's founders tested the demand for textbook rentals, they discovered an earned secret: students would pay relatively high prices to rent textbooks. The ability for Chegg to get higher profit margins for its textbook rentals convinced investors to back them in their next round of financing. This financing provided the capital to develop a functioning platform for orders, shipping, and inventory management.

Okta's founders presented unfinished Balsamiq prototypes. In each situation, these prototypes were intentionally disposable, not the final product. This ephemeral nature isn't a flaw but a feature. By accepting the fleeting life of the early prototypes, innovators make space for relentless iteration without the emotional weight of discarding a completed product. The goal? Constant discovery, without looking back.

All these circumstances point to the value of timeboxing, a time-management technique where you allocate a fixed amount of time, or a "box" of time, to a specific activity or task—in this case, prototype development. Once the allocated time has expired, the activity is considered complete, whether or not it has been finished. The purpose is to ensure that you stay focused on a task, prevent procrastination, and help manage time more efficiently by limiting the duration spent on a particular task.

The aim is to quickly validate if there's genuine demand for your idea. Engaging with potential users early and often with tangible implementation ideas speeds this up. Some start-ups hesitate to do this, often because they silently fear that no one may desperately want a product that embodies their insight. Ultimately, in a start-up, there is a huge cultural difference between finding any number of desperate customers versus zero desperate customers. Many start-ups have a huge theoretical market opportunity but never find a single customer desperate for what they propose to build.

DON'T SETTLE

Most start-up ideas that seem alluring at first won't be worth your time as a founder. If that weren't the case, there would be far more breakthroughs. Before you decide to cross the Rubicon and pursue an idea, you should hold it to a high standard. Don't settle. If you haven't found an idea that meets your standards, you don't need to pursue it. Implementation prototypes, combined with the stress tests of inflections and insights, can help you eliminate ideas that are seductive on the surface but not powerful enough, while also giving you the courage to explore ideas that seem crazy to most (and maybe even to you!) but that have the elements that can lead to breakthroughs.

When refining your prototype, it's crucial to collaborate with the right individuals. Many are content with the status quo and might not resonate with your vision. They will not like any implementation you show them because they are not ready to embrace your insight. Instead, focus on a select group who deeply connect with your future insights. I refer to these individuals as "co-conspirators" because they share your beliefs and see the potential. We'll now dive deeper into the importance of identifying and understanding these early supporters.

10

CO-CONSPIRATORS

Recruiting Your Start-Up Team

*Alright, here's the deal. You're gonna need a crew as nuts
as you are. Who do you got in mind?*
—FROM THE 2001 MOVIE OCEAN'S ELEVEN

Your breakthrough idea is meaningless if you can't convince
people to embrace it with you to make it real. But there's an
extra challenge here. Pattern-breaking start-ups offer a provocative point of view about the future that defies the norm. They
break away from conventional wisdom, challenging traditional
beliefs and methods. They argue for a bold, different approach
that clashes with today's status quo. The type of help you'll need
is different from business as usual. To champion such a radical
idea, you need true believers, including your start-up team, initial customers and collaborators, and even investors. These people

should passionately believe in the transformation you envision and feel personally empowered to help you make it happen. You want to enlist others to embrace your outsider or underdog perspective rather than insiders seeking mainstream approval or prestige. You want people who will rally together in a way that builds deep camaraderie and passionate commitment to defeat the incumbents, not people who view this as just a job with potential upside if things work out. You want pirates, not people motivated to join the navy.

You need co-conspirators.

Most people don't want to sign up for something like this. They're either comfortable with the status quo, or worse yet, they're motivated to protect it. Co-conspirators will not only be rabid believers in your insight; they'll help you overcome the pushback your movement will encounter from nonbelievers in its early days.

Breakthrough start-ups succeed by animating the beliefs of the right co-conspirators, beginning with your start-up team. They need to think, feel, and act differently than employees and managers at a normal business.

ALL THAT JAZZ

A normal business is like a marching band in which people need specific dance steps and sheet music to operate effectively. They want to perform with consistency. But building a start-up isn't like operating a normal company. It has very few standard ways of doing things, and it seeks to create something that the world has never seen before. Normal organizations can't do this. A breakthrough start-up shouldn't begin by populating boxes in a traditional organizational chart.

Breakthrough start-ups behave less like marching bands and more like improv jazz bands. In the French Quarter in New Orleans, you can see them up close. The leader starts an improvisational riff. The rest of the band picks up on his cue, and moves with him to create, on the spot, a unique live performance. An improv jazz ensemble will never perform exactly that way again. It is a one-off—the result of people who read each other's cues rather than sheet music.

Think of it this way: Suppose you hire someone from a highly regarded larger company. Their initial inclination is to introduce a process familiar to them from their former workplace. This is usually a sign that you've hired the wrong person. Processes exist at larger companies to implement the marching-band sheet music that drives their success at scale. Your start-up needs people who can execute at the tempo and in the manner of an improv jazz band.

You also want people who aren't motivated by status in the organization. Management in big companies requires clear chains of command, processes, and boundaries of accountability. But start-up teams want—and need—everyone to bring every ounce of their creative essence to the task at hand, rather than being subservient to the team's organizational structure. These are people who all feel the rhythm and can riff on it—who thrive on chaos. Emmett Shear of Twitch paints a vivid picture of this intense, often tumultuous energy: "We were horrendously dysfunctional. We had a six-hour argument about whether to put military time or an 'AM/PM' next to timestamps in our chat interface. But start-ups don't win because of excellent management. If they did, there wouldn't be any successful start-ups. The big companies would crush them. Start-ups succeed because you have smart people who are willing to work very hard and run into and over obstacles again and again. And in the early days, nobody cares about your start-up anyway, so the consequences of screwing up aren't that great. You've got nothing to lose. You have no users; there's no one to hurt. As you get bigger, the rules change. Then you must care about screwing up, because if you screw up, that's millions of people you've affected."

As a four-person founding team, the Twitch founders navigated through continual and chaotic interactions and decisions. But the glue binding them was a level of determination, mutual respect, and trust rarely seen in larger organizations. They shared a collective tenacity, an unwillingness to concede, irrespective of the errors or hurdles they faced. This shared determination was their anchor even during the worst of times. Emmett continues, "At no point was I afraid that we would lose our friendship over any of that dysfunction. . . . We all respected each other, and we had our own areas of ownership."

When you build your team, take your inspiration from the film *Ocean's Eleven*, the 2001 heist blockbuster featuring a team comprising a safecracker, a gymnast, a con man, a demolition expert, a guy to shut down the power grid, and a getaway driver—an ensemble of people with a combination of skills and mutual trust in Danny Ocean, played by George Clooney. They all believe that they can steal every last dollar in the "unbreakable safe" at the Bellagio Hotel. Of course, in your start-up, you're not actually trying to commit a crime (though normal people might not see it that way!). You don't need safecrackers and getaway drivers. But it helps to have the skills, the mutual trust, and the energy inspired by being in on a conspiracy together, because changing the future has a subversive element to it.

The Twitch founders embodied the traits of the *Ocean's Eleven* team. Each member brought distinct yet complementary skills to the table, and there were minimal conflicts over roles or task ownership. They took lots of risks, in their case largely because they had so little to lose. They had few resources in the form of capital and people, so they had to be inventive in their approaches to getting things done. This is similar to how the *Ocean's Eleven* team had to be inventive in their approach to the heist. Like Danny Ocean's crew, when confronted with unexpected challenges, the Twitch team didn't waver; they grew more resilient. An informal sense of trust formed the bedrock of their collaborations. Both the Twitch team and the *Ocean's Eleven* crew depended on one another during intense moments, relying on each member's expertise and dedication. At its essence, *Ocean's Eleven* is an underdog story where a smaller, less powerful group takes on the big, established player (the casino). Emmett Shear's narrative underscores Twitch's self-perception as a resolute underdog, unyielding in the face of doubts and obstacles.

BUILDING YOUR TEAM OF CO-CONSPIRATORS
Exactly what kinds of people and skills you'll need depends on the future you're trying to create and what you're trying to build. The best practices involved in start-up hiring could fill the pages of an entire book. That said, we have observed some specific approaches that contribute to success in pattern-breaking outcomes when building a start-up team of breakthrough co-conspirators.

Hire to Take Out Key Risks

Creating a breakthrough start-up is risky. Survival depends on identifying the biggest risks you face and gathering the people who can take out the risks, one by one. You need to bring on cofounders or hire people early with the skills and audacity to minimize those risks. If a change in the law could put you out of business, you need somebody on your team or in your orbit who can head that off. If you're SpaceX, you need people who can build rockets that can blast into outer space, land back on the launchpad, and be reused. If you're building a new social media platform, you need somebody on your team who is a fanatic about nailing distribution. Scaling users is the biggest risk you face, so your distribution is key.

Emphasize Chemistry

Consummate trust among your start-up co-conspirators is also vital. Such trust often stems from long-term friendships or from having worked together on projects under very intense circumstances. Having experience working together matters enormously, especially for cofounders. I'm not a big fan of so-called founder dating—websites and mixers designed for the purpose of meeting prospective cofounders. Sometimes that works, but often it doesn't. Too many people on the team discover that they have different values or unresolved tensions when they're in the crucible. Founder disputes are one of the top early start-up killers, and they outnumber investor-founder disputes. Garry Tan, current president of Y Combinator, describes the situation well: "Posterous, the start-up I co-founded in 2008, grew 10X yearly and became a top 200 Quantcast website in that time. But by the end of 2010, growth had flatlined. When things were going well, we were too busy keeping the site online to have anything to disagree about. I learned the hard way that if you haven't prepared for conflict in your co-founder relationship, you'll be at each other's throats right at the moment when you most need to be working well together. When the honeymoon ended, there was no healthy foundation to support the company."

Successful cofounders, even if they are friends, need to develop the chemistry to embrace conflict rather than avoiding it. Their collaboration should be strongest when times are toughest.

And while friendship and trust are necessary for good team chemistry, they aren't sufficient. If you bring together friends with similar skills and interests but they start arguing over whose job it is to do what, that's trouble too. Matthew Prince is the cofounder of Cloudflare, which plays a pivotal role in enhancing the performance and security of millions of websites and online services. He emphasizes that if you have the right start-up collaborators, there's never an argument about roles. If you have arguments about roles or make compromises like having co-CEOs so that two founders share the same responsibilities, then either you've built the wrong team or you're not facing important unresolved issues about trusting your cofounder to do his or her job. As a founder, you're trying to bring together people who believe in the future you envision as deeply as you do, with complementary skills, a clear sense of their roles, and deep-seated trust.

I'm not suggesting that you and your co-conspirators need to agree on everything. Some of the great start-up teams I've known argued plenty. The Justin.tv team had arguments about branding, what features to prioritize, how to monetize without alienating users, growth strategies, moderation, and content policies. Despite these differences of opinion, I had the sense that there wasn't much unresolved tension among them. It's the right kind of disagreement. It's not as if they were angry at each other's existence. They knew each other's strengths and weaknesses, and how to work around their blind spots. No one felt the need to suppress their ideas or concerns to stay in their own lane. Everybody showed up as their complete and actual self, committed to the same goal. That kind of mutual understanding is hard to build without some type of working history.

It's also important to note that even if you have been friends for a long time, you need to work on nurturing the relationship at all points along the way. Working as a team to perpetrate an optimistic conspiracy to change the future takes a lot out of everybody involved, even more than at conventional start-ups, which are hard on people in the first place. Returning to Garry Tan's example at Posterous, he points out, "In my case, I had known my co-founder for more than eight years, and we had been friends since college. We had history, but we learned history is not enough—you've got to maintain it like any relationship. It isn't enough that you've been friends for years. It matters what your relationship is like now."

Find Your Superbuilder

A start-up faces so much uncertainty that the ability to build whatever unexpected thing comes up next is invaluable. One pattern I've noticed in breakthrough start-ups is that they have a "superbuilder" on their team. When—not if—something about your first idea is wrong, the superbuilder helps you move rapidly in the direction of what's right because he or she is not constrained in technical flexibility.

As I pointed out earlier in recounting the Airbnb story, one of the things I missed was its superbuilder, Nate Blecharczyk. I spent time in my meeting focused on Brian Chesky, on the cereal boxes, and on all the things that went wrong with their demo. I never took the time to figure out Nate's capabilities. As it turned out, Nate's ability to build whatever was necessary is an unsung aspect of Airbnb's epic tale of success. Nate created a Google AdWords hack that allowed them to target specific people in specific cities. He built one-click integration that allowed Airbnb hosts to get their listings viewed by Craigslist's millions of users, which was a clever hack. You might recall from our earlier story about Airbnb that they were able to leverage Facebook Connect, which was an application programming interface (API) that allowed other companies to communicate with the Facebook platform directly from their programs. Airbnb used Facebook Connect's API to streamline user registration, foster trust via mutual connections, autofill profile details, enable social sharing, and leverage friend recommendations, all of which promoted platform growth. But Craigslist didn't have a public API. So Nate found a workaround that cleverly integrated with Craigslist, allowing hosts to autopost their Airbnb listings. The tactic pushed the boundaries of platform etiquette and terms of use, and Craigslist eventually made changes to prevent this kind of automated cross-posting. By that time, Airbnb had already gained substantial traction. Nate took on and solved a series of additional major technical challenges, from payments to customer service, reviews, and more—and at first, he was the only person on the team with the ability to do it.

In the early days of a start-up, the superbuilder might be as important as the start-up leader, and they're most likely not the same person. Superbuilders bring to the task a set of complementary creative capabilities that can't be replaced or duplicated.

A superbuilder doesn't just bring expertise; she accelerates a team's pace, sometimes making the difference between the company's success and failure. The early days of Justin.tv/Twitch provided a prime example of this. Michael Seibel, a Justin.tv cofounder, shared a particularly tense experience from those days. Many users were streaming copyrighted content on Justin.tv, including major sporting events. When NBC invested heavily in streaming rights for the 2008 Beijing Olympics, the network was determined to protect its investment. Seibel recalls, "We got a Friday afternoon call on my cell phone from a lawyer for NBC. She was letting us know that on Monday, they would go to the court in San Francisco and have our website shut down for the entire month so that nobody could broadcast any Olympics on Justin.tv. This wasn't just about stopping Olympic broadcasts; a month-long shutdown could have killed the platform. Justin.tv might be out of business."

Facing this existential threat, Seibel inquired about possible solutions. The lawyer mentioned YouTube's special software that NBC was using to monitor and take down copyright-infringing content. Seibel proposed, "What if we built something similar for you over the weekend?"

Despite the attorney's skepticism that it could be accomplished that quickly, the team worked relentlessly during the weekend. By Sunday morning, they presented their solution to NBC. After testing it, NBC decided not to pursue shutting down Justin.tv and opted to use the tool instead.

This example underscores the crucial role a superbuilder can play during a crisis. But as Seibel notes, the essence of a superbuilder goes deeper. He remarks, "One of the most important characteristics of the builder that I think people miss is faith. The superbuilder has the faith to build things they never built before. Kyle Vogt was a canonical example of this, even more so than Emmett Shear. Emmett had a certain degree of confidence, but Kyle thought he could build anything. And it turns out that he pretty much could."

Interestingly, after the experience at Justin.tv/Twitch, Kyle Vogt founded Cruise Automation, a company focused on autonomous vehicles. His passion for this challenge dated back to his MIT days. I met Kyle in the early stages of Cruise, and I considered investing in his start-up. Most of our team at Floodgate were skeptical. Trusting my instincts, I invested anyway. Less than a year later, GM acquired Cruise for over $1 billion.

Superbuilders play an important role in attracting other co-conspirators to the team, along with customers and partners, because they bring to life the technical artistry behind the insights in a way that excites people who care about technical excellence.

Today we live in a world where you can get stuff built anywhere. You can specify a product and then go to an online service like Fiverr or Upwork to find a freelance coder, or hire contractors from places with lower expenses such as Eastern Europe. You can get your product built for much less than you'd pay an employee in New York City, Los Angeles, or Silicon Valley. But when you're a start-up, it's not about the cost of building things. It's about the ability to build anything that's required to create a breakthrough, and to build it as fast as you can. No team of outsourced developers with a distant relationship to the company could have delivered the weekend turnaround that saved Justin.tv. You would have to send them an email, and they'd have to fully understand the spec in advance. But this was a situation where rapid and radical improvisation was required, and it couldn't be completely specified upfront. If you tried to subcontract this work, you'd probably get a first-pass attempt a day later if people were even willing to work through the weekend. It wouldn't be quite right, and you'd need to iterate again . . . right into oblivion.

Find Great Undiscovered Talent

I've never met a start-up founding team that didn't say, "It's all about the people." I've met far fewer teams who hired as if their lives depended on it. They should—because hiring is a matter of your start-up's life or death. I believe the best founders devote 15 to 20 percent of their time to hiring, whether they have openings or not.

Keith Rabois played a crucial role in defining and implementing PayPal's government relations and dealing with regulatory issues. Keith is a well-known alumnus of the renowned "PayPal Mafia," a group of former PayPal employees who went on to establish and develop many influential technology companies and investment firms after leaving PayPal. Since his PayPal days he has also played key roles at LinkedIn, Slide, and Square and is now a partner at the venture capital firm Founders Fund. Keith has profound insights on team building and emphasizes a vital point about the process of finding the very best: you have to find great undiscovered talent. Why? Because by the time someone's great and discovered, it's very difficult to recruit them to your start-up—and they might not even be cut out for life in your jazz band.

Here are five factors to think about when you seek out great undiscovered talent:

1. Recruit all the time. When you need to hire someone, you'll have a huge head start.
2. Learn to recognize great talent. A great start-up employee is tenacious, learns quickly without instruction, is incredibly resourceful, thrives in a chaotic, unpredictable environment—and is out to prove something.
3. Match the need. When you need upside, hire for aptitude. When you're protecting against the downside, hire for experience.
4. Maintain an Undiscovered Awesome People (UAP) list. Ask each of your co-conspirators to make a list of at least ten people who have the traits to be effective in a start-up, and do this exercise yourself too. Even if they aren't a good fit now, they might be later—so keep in touch.
5. Sell your start-up in public, all the time. When you talk to potential recruits for your start-up team, notice the parts of your vision they find most compelling—these are likely the parts you should emphasize in your overall marketing efforts. Likewise, use the pitch that works with customers to draw in potential recruits. You want to tell your start-up's true story and bring others into the fold. Founders like Whitney Wolfe Herd from Bumble and Austen Allred of Bloom Institute of Technology attract recruits with the same ease that they attract

customers. And then there is Elon Musk, arguably one of the best at selling his vision in both marketing and recruiting. He hasn't spent a dime on traditional marketing or advertising for his companies. Still, many say he's unsurpassed at getting the word out and drawing in the world's brightest talent.

It is essential to build a team of internal co-conspirators. You'll need external co-conspirators too—investors and early-believing customers who will help propagate your movement. That's the focus of the next chapter.

11

YOUR FIRST TRUE BELIEVERS

Attracting the Perfect Customers and Investors

> *We're a couple of misfits*
> *We're a couple of misfits*
> *What's the matter with misfits*
> *That's where we fit in!*
> —Rudolph the Red-Nosed Reindeer
> and the Island of Misfit Toys

Most people living in the present won't be believers when they first hear about your insight. Most won't like the future you describe because, whether they recognize it or not, they personify the present fighting back. Your challenge is to find the limited subset of people who do believe in your future and then convince them to join you there.

EARLY CUSTOMERS NEED TO BE BELIEVERS

These first believers are your external co-conspirators. Like your internal ones, they are kindred spirits attracted by belief, not utility, to the future you inhabit. The most important thing to recognize about early believers is that more isn't necessarily better. You shouldn't think of your earliest efforts as a generic sales funnel where you throw as many people as possible in at the top to maximize the number who come out at the bottom as customers. It might seem counterintuitive, but you must choose your first believers with care rather than getting merely anyone to choose you. The right believers will form the heart of your movement, leading the world toward a new future that you build together. The wrong believers will push you toward the conventional, drag you back to the present, and cause you to drift from your desired future. And the nonbelievers will just waste your time.

Early customers are not simply people who buy what you're selling. They're motivated by belief—belief in the world that you've articulated in your story. You want each iteration of your start-up idea to validate their beliefs so they will spread the word to more and more early believers who adopt your story.

The original Tesla Roadster wouldn't have survived a comparison with any mainstream luxury car of the same price: it had a body borrowed from Lotus, and its radio and seats looked like they came from a standard parts bin. Tesla faced comparably priced cars whose features included ten-way adjustable seats and ten-speaker, five-hundred-watt audio systems.

Did any of that matter? No. Tesla's founding team got an A-plus in the one thing that did matter, which was demonstrating to people who shared their passion for electric cars that it was actually possible to build such a product—and such a car company. They found believers in the mission, defied the doubters and naysayers who didn't matter, and touched something deep in the hearts of those who had bought in. The Roadster was a breakthrough in the eyes of Tesla's first believers, and that was enough.

The original Tesla Roadster wasn't just a minimum viable product; it was a minimum viable future. It was a functioning prototype of a future early customers found compelling. Wealthy people bought a Roadster because it validated their beliefs. And when they drove their Roadsters, they signaled their belief in that future for others to see. If Tesla had conducted a "normal" focus group or treated all customer input as if it were equal, they would have focused on improving the features that didn't matter as much to the first believers who were prepared to be co-conspirators. The first believers didn't care about "normal" car features. They didn't want better versions of those things. They wanted something that was radically different in a way that validated their belief in the story behind Tesla's mission statement.

But there's no single minimum viable future. They vary, based on the future you're trying to create and what it takes to validate the beliefs of your early believers. If you're Todd McKinnon and Freddy Kerrest of Okta, and you're trying to create a cloud identity-management platform, you can't just wave your hands or ask your early customers to use their imaginations. The first iteration of Okta had to enable its early believers to show their organizations that it could provide a common interface for access to multiple cloud services they cared about. Okta's initial believers were innovative customers who had embraced the cloud early, but they also had a practical problem in need of a practical solution.

Okta needed to show early believers that it could deliver enough demonstrable utility in solving their pain to validate their beliefs so they would stay in the relationship.

Marc Andreessen and Eric Bina built the Mosaic browser before the days of search engines or other capabilities we take for granted with today's internet. To get to a website, you had to know how to look for it, or it had to be a link on Mosaic's home page. Creating web pages in those early days required understanding HTML and having access to a web server to host the content. The World Wide Web was still in its infancy, so the number of web pages was relatively small. The community of web developers was a tight-knit, innovative group, often called "alpha geeks." They were mainly academics and researchers, and word spread of their excitement through various channels: academic networks, Usenet, word of mouth, conferences, workshops, and early online publications. Alpha geeks didn't promote Mosaic primarily for business reasons; they found pleasure in the joy and simplicity of tinkering with it. As word of Mosaic's potential spread, the number of web pages and creators grew rapidly. The movement was a bottom-up phenomenon, driven by the thrill of those who reveled in its new, empowering capabilities.

You might remember that in the late 1970s, the original Apple computer found favor with another group of alpha geeks, the sort that tinkered in garages and gathered in home-brew clubs. Those early enthusiasts respected the craft of cofounder Steve Wozniak, specifically, his way of making circuit boards simply designed but deeply functional. The early personal computer was like a blank canvas, waiting to be programmed for the next task. It could connect to a person's home TV, and it could load the BASIC programming language from a cassette. Enthusiasts could enhance their computer with additional memory, various input/output ports, and expansion slots, creating a buzz about its potential. This excitement also fostered a community, notably in the Homebrew Computer Club, of which Wozniak was a member. All the members shared Wozniak's spirit of innovation and his DIY attitude toward personal computing, fueling a grassroots surge toward a very different future.

With Tesla, Elon Musk targeted affluent people who wanted a functioning prototype of his radically different future. With SpaceX, he targeted the US government, which had money to invest in the advancement of space travel and commercialized space opportunities—provided officials believed SpaceX could deliver. Ultimately, even NASA was persuaded that it could benefit from helping the best minds in private industry advance its agenda of extending the reach of humanity into space. It wasn't about getting an immediate return on investment. SpaceX was NASA's way of pushing the envelope—of taking risks that weren't as easy for a large government agency to take on its own—with the efficiency and effectiveness that an agile start-up could offer.

In the early days, you want to select your early believers, rather than the other way around. For Okta, the right first believers had to believe in the cloud. They had already implemented Salesforce and other cloud apps and were experiencing the problem of their users struggling to remember how to log in to all of them securely. Perhaps these early adopters of the cloud had already tried to solve the problem themselves.

In the early days of Airbnb, CEO Brian Chesky began knocking on the doors of the initial group of hosts. He took to the streets of New York, the first place with meaningful numbers of early users. One host stood out. He greeted Brian with a notebook filled with thoughts he had compiled to improve the platform. That's the type of first true believer you're looking for!

The challenge is to recognize a visionary customer when you meet one. The visionary customer is likely not living in the present; they are one of the few who live in the future. For people living in the future, their first encounter with your product clicks with their view of what's to come. Like fellow inhabitants of the Island of Misfit Toys, they have been waiting for your idea, perhaps without fully realizing it. They might be thinking (or saying out loud), "Where have you been? This is what the future will be like." These people are poised to co-create the future with you. It's a great blessing to encounter them and a tragic mistake to overlook their potential to help you find a quicker path to greatness.

Conversely, as a founder, it's easy to fall into the trap of talking to any customer who will give you the time of day. After all, they may buy your product, and they are eager to tell you what they think about it. Be wary of this, because heeding the words of those who live in the present will divert you from the future you're trying to create. It would have been counterproductive for Tesla to take the advice to make ten-way adjustable seats for the original Roadster. It's important for you to focus on only the customers who can accelerate your path to building what's missing in the future.

EARLY INVESTORS ALSO NEED TO BE BELIEVERS

Potential customers are not created equal. Neither are potential investors. You're going to hear "no" more than you hear "yes"—and (though it seems counterintuitive) that's what you want to hear when you're on the right track.

The world of raising venture capital is one of the most murky and misunderstood fields I've encountered in my business career. When I first started spending time in the venture business, I had been a founder or executive at back-to-back start-ups that went public. We had raised money from some of the top people in the business, including Jim Breyer, one of the most successful venture capitalists in history. And yet when I first started spending time on "the other side of the table" as a seed-stage venture capitalist, I realized how little I really knew about fundraising, much less how the venture business works.

Understanding these things would have helped me a lot as a founder, particularly with early-stage investors, who are best viewed as another type of co-conspirator rather than just a means to raise money to get started. This is especially true if you are pursuing a non-consensus idea that can lead to a breakthrough.

Many founders make the mistake of believing that fundraising is like a sales cycle. They think you need to develop a funnel of VC prospects. Then they create a slide presentation that incorporates advice from people who want to see them succeed. The problem with this approach is that it falls into a different version of the same trap: selling to normal people.

A raw start-up has two things: the start-up team and the insight. Just as you want an early start-up team and customers who buy into your insight and want to co-create a different future with you, you need the same in your early investors. It's hard to internalize this idea at first. A lot of founders feel like it's a bad sign if most VCs dislike their start-up ideas. But in my experience, it's far better if a handful of VCs say, "Where have you been all my life?" once they understand your insight. In the beginning, it's better to attract a fanatical few investors rather than a large number who are only moderately interested in what you are doing.

Ultimately, investors believe or they don't believe. If they don't believe at first, you won't convince them until you've proven yourself in the future. You should move on. It's a mistake to focus a lot of energy on a pitch to nonbelievers. You muddle the message when you spend time with someone who's simply not ready to be a co-conspirator. Worse, you muddle the message for the people you should be spending time with when you attempt to accommodate the objections of those who aren't ready to believe in the first place. This problem is similar to the curse of too many benefits when talking to early customer co-conspirators, a topic we addressed in Chapter 9.

I've seen this muddling firsthand. To understand how it happens, picture this scenario: Your start-up gears up to secure funding, and you craft your initial pitch deck. You already have a few angel investors, mentors, and supporters. Naturally, you seek their input.

An adviser suggests tailoring the pitch to the latest buzzwords in VC circles. So instead of simply stating, "We're Airbnb. We let you rent out an extra room in your house," your adviser persuades you to shift to something like, "We're Airbnb, a residential real estate marketplace." The adviser's rationale is that "marketplaces" have network effects, and VCs love the economics and upside of network effects.

Another confidant asserts that you should paint the big picture first before plunging into the details. Before diving into your core concept, you might spotlight Millennial trends, the shift to online shopping, the rise of social platforms, and the changing attitudes toward hospitality brands. The intent? To underscore how your potential is in tune with current macro trends.

Yet another mentor recommends casting a wider net, hinting at a vast market beyond your initial customer base. To do justice to this broader vision, you'll need a few more slides.

Further feedback suggests infusing the pitch with more bullet points that contain certain investor-friendly terms. So those get sprinkled in. The deck swells, accommodating every well-intentioned piece of feedback.

Now it's time for real-world presentations to investors. But the presentations aren't home runs. Rejection emails offer varied feedback: unclear business model, ambiguous unit economics, raising too much money, raising too little money. You tweak the deck after each critique. Your presentation balloons, but at least it now has a slide for each likely objection. I call these overloaded presentations "Frankendecks." They attempt to address every potential question or counterargument, but this approach dilutes the main message. Much like Frankenstein was a patchwork of parts, these decks lose their cohesive narrative about your vision for the future.

A new challenge emerges. Pitch meetings feel rushed because you need to be able to get through all your slides and make all your points in a limited time window. Minutes tick away, leaving only brief moments to demo your product or share user testimonials. Questions in the meeting feel like they distract from your ability to get all your points across in the allotted time, so you rush your answers to stay on point.

I could continue, but you probably see where I'm going. This is an example of the muddle I described earlier. When you approach investors this way, the insight that drives the start-up opportunity—the real signal—gets lost in the noise. Even people who are ready to be co-conspirators get confused. And those who aren't ready give yet another objection that contributes to even more noise that creates self-doubt in the founders.

Rather than viewing your pitch this way, it's good to consider an alternative framing. As far as you're concerned, in the early days there are two types of investors that exist in the world: those who are ready to believe your insight and those who aren't. Only the first type matters. The second type does not.

Your biggest potential mistake is failing to make your vision super clear for those ready to back your groundbreaking insight. They are your potential co-conspirators. Yet when the moment comes for them to share your vision, they get lost in the haze of overwhelming detail or indirect language. They need help understanding why they should be your first true believers.

Potential co-conspirators crave a sharp, direct pitch. They want you to explain what you are doing, quickly, and with straight talk. They want you to dive into the demo and offer a compelling, concise description rather than a vague one that says everything but ultimately nothing. They want relatable stories of genuine users and why they are desperate for your solution.

I've been in too many meetings where twenty minutes fly by and I'm still in the dark about what the start-up even does. I empathize with why this happens. It's hard to get a pitch right, and VCs often bring far less than their A game to pitch meetings. Maybe they're distracted by another issue with one of their existing portfolio companies. But here's a plea: don't let the muddle happen to you.

Founders should treat every investor like a potential partner in crime, and they should pitch with that mindset. If an investor remains unmoved, don't see it as a challenge to overcome—see it as a sign. Time to move on. Seek that kindred spirit who shares your vision, believes in your mission, and genuinely cares. Don't solve for the nonbelievers. For now, they don't matter.

The right VCs to engage are the ones you want to talk to as you stress-test your insight. They reveal themselves through the start-ups they back, the language on their websites, and what they say online. In approaching them, you're sincere in the idea that you're not selling them or trying to anticipate and sell around their potential objections. You're really trading ideas in the realm of your insight. If you have done the work it takes to develop an insight, you'll attract the VCs you care about and repel the nonbelievers. I encourage the founders I work with to begin with something like this: "Before I get too far with this pitch, I need to tell you about my belief in the future that is nonobvious, and why I think I'm right. If you conclude at any point that you disagree with this, nothing else I say will make sense to you, and I can give you the rest of your time back."

When you think about it, it's inspiring to realize that most investors should disagree with you, and that this is part of the process of coming up with a breakthrough idea. When you grasp that the goal of fundraising is to spend all your energy on people who are willing to entertain your true advantages—the things that create the conditions for your breakthrough—it follows that the objections of nonbelievers shouldn't keep you up at night.

The best start-ups I've seen have a set of co-conspirators who all believe the same insight and go to battle together to convince the nonbelievers of the world that they're right. Everyone involved—the team, early customers, and investors—share the right kind of crazy. This is the energy you want. Spend your time with the people who value your advantage, and don't waste your energy and angst on those who aren't ready to move. My business partner Ann exemplified the desired mindset in her relationship with Lyft's founders. When Logan Green and John Zimmer spoke of the anticipated legal troubles ahead of their launch, Ann didn't flinch, asking, "Do you think people will love this product?" The unwavering confidence in Logan and John's response convinced Ann to throw her full support behind their cause without hesitation.

Ann summarizes it like a true co-conspirator: "You don't reach greatness by figuring out all the things that can go wrong. You do it by figuring out how things can go right."

BUILD YOUR ECOSYSTEM WITH CO-CONSPIRATORS

Just as the status quo has an ecosystem of customers, competitors, partners, buyers, and suppliers, it takes a coalition of people and a well-defined ecosystem to support a breakthrough. Think of Tesla's charging stations, its Gigafactory in Texas, or the supply chain required to build a car. If any link in that ecosystem were missing, Tesla's movement would be severely limited in its ability to spread.

Building an ecosystem to support a new idea is actually nothing new. Here's a classic, old-school example of a breakthrough founder: Clarence Birdseye in the 1920s. Birdseye was in the

Arctic watching the Aleutian Islanders fish. When they caught a fish, they would flash freeze it in the snow. Why? Because they didn't want to eat all the fish on the day they caught them; they wanted to save some for the future.

Birdseye went home wondering whether he could apply flash freezing to fruits, vegetables, and meat. He experimented and found that he could. If all Birdseye had done was deliver a box of frozen food, he would've failed. He had to persuade railroad companies to develop freezer cars to transport his products from his factory to grocery stores, and grocery stores to install freezers on their premises to store his products.

Clarence Birdseye is the reason that supermarkets have frozen-food aisles today. He understood that to realize the value proposition of his insight, he needed to create an ecosystem before his idea could become real. It wasn't enough just to offer the end product; he had to offer a viable set of integrated components that would enable the future he saw. And he had to turn all these people into his early co-conspirators. He had to give all of them a clear call to action. They all had to move together to build the ecosystem for his product.

Tesla also had to build out its ecosystem as it expanded its product line. The Model S that followed Tesla's Roadster was a more comfortable and practical sedan, and Tesla's believers began to multiply. Then Tesla introduced Superchargers—the charging stations that made Teslas more practical because they began to eliminate driver anxiety about the car having limited range. The Model 3 was meaningfully less expensive than the S, and the believers multiplied again. With each step, Tesla's movement appealed to more people who became believers, and now the industry's giants are scrambling to join Elon Musk in a future that's played by his rules.

It's an astonishing achievement. And it illustrates a critical point: it's the founder's job to bridge the gap between the present and the future. If people aren't moving to the future the founder inhabits, it's up to the founder to spend more time with those who are ready to move, or to be more effective in giving the right people reasons to move, or some combination of both.

I meet founders who lament the fact that too few people (customers, investors, or partners) see what they see. It's not enough to say, "I wish everyone could see what I see, but they can't." That's a cop-out. If people don't move to your future, then your future won't happen. If they're not moving, it's an indication that either the inflections, or the insight, or the idea, or the story you're telling about the future isn't powerful enough, or else the story isn't aimed at the right people.

With time, founders build movements by pulling more and more people toward the future they inhabit. Authors such as Geoffrey Moore have written insightfully about how this customer-adoption life cycle works for breakthrough products. With each step they take, breakthrough founders compel more believers to join the movement. Eventually, adoption reaches a tipping point, and normal people start joining the movement as well.

When this happens, your start-up's insight becomes an accepted truth instead of a heresy, and your business makes the transition from a start-up to a company. Then you are the incumbent, and you define the rules. Of course, that's not the end of the story—because the cycle of business life has no end. Just watch out for the next breakthrough that seeks to overturn your hard-won success, because it's coming!

The notion of moving people to the future raises another aspect of making breakthroughs real. For early co-conspirators to move to the future that you've designed, you must *move* them—which is where the power of movements comes into play. We'll dig into that topic next.

12

LAUNCHING YOUR MOVEMENT

Overturning the Status Quo

*The people who are crazy enough to think they can
change the world are the ones that do.*
—STEVE JOBS, VISIONARY COFOUNDER OF APPLE

I deas make radical change possible. Movements make radical change real. The elements of inflection theory that we've discussed so far—inflection, insight, and idea—create the potential for radical change. But creating a potential breakthrough isn't enough. You have to take the next step and make the potential actual by changing how people behave. Creating a movement is the process of converting a potential breakthrough into an actual breakthrough.

WHAT IS A MOVEMENT?

Without a movement you're standing in the future alone with a radical idea that changes the rules of what's possible and gives people new capabilities. You need to pull real people in the real world toward the future you're living in.

It's not easy. The real world has big incumbent companies and multitudes of people with ingrained habits. The incumbents have a lot of things figured out, and they have abundant assets to help them maintain their positions of dominance in the present. They're embedded in an ecosystem with partners and others who share a vested interest in keeping things just as they are. And as if that isn't a big-enough obstacle to overcome, we all know that customer habits are hard to change.

By contrast, you have no products or customers yet, and very few material resources. It will stay that way unless you devise a strategy to change how people think, feel, and act, so that they become your users or customers and embrace the beliefs embodied in your insight.

The conventional approach of going to market assumes that there is a market, and that your goal is to gain share in that market by being better than the competition or by covering white space that incumbents haven't. But no matter how well you do this, you will continue competing according to the established rules—rules that were designed to give incumbents an advantage. As a result, you never escape comparison with them.

If you want to create a breakthrough, the best strategy is to avoid competing with incumbents at all. Instead, it is far better to change the rules entirely. Changing the rules and starting a movement is how you avoid the comparison trap.

A movement is a group of people with a shared belief in moving together toward a different future.

People typically think of movements as social or political, such as Martin Luther King Jr. and civil rights. Movements such as these succeed because they appeal to, animate, and activate people's beliefs, while also introducing a mechanism that empowers the underdog to defeat the entrenched status quo. The civil rights movement appealed to people's beliefs that the status quo in race relations needed to change, while introducing the mechanism of nonviolent resistance to show the terrible injustices of the status quo.

Movements are organized to work outside the established system to create radical change. Within social systems, special interest groups typically work from the inside to create incremental reforms. Radical changes, however, come from revolutionaries operating outside the established system. Their position as outsiders has taught them that they need to engage in different tactics because they lack the resources and the access to the system enjoyed by special interest groups.

The business world can be viewed through the same lens.

Most start-ups act more like interest groups than revolutionaries. They work within the existing system of business and offer something that's an improvement over existing ways of going about life. Breakthrough start-ups are the revolutionaries who seek to overthrow the status quo and create fundamentally new ways of going about life. Breakthrough movements turn the perceived strengths of the status quo into sources of discontent.

Founders who successfully create a movement take the assets, advantages, and assumptions of the status quo—the strengths enjoyed by incumbents—and turn them into the incumbents' greatest weaknesses, just as judo masters use their opponents' size and strength against them. They force incumbents to apologize for their strengths rather than emphasizing them.

Consider again the story of Airbnb. The status quo for Airbnb was hotels, which have a lot of things going for them. When you stay at one, you know what to expect. A stay at the Marriott in Austin will offer a similar level of service quality and overall atmosphere as a Marriott in San Francisco or even Paris. Marriott has spent decades perfecting its ability to provide this uniformity of service, and they do it well. What is the weakness in this strength? It's precisely that the hotel experience in all three cities is similar.

Airbnb's founders reframed the choices about lodging in a way that makes this similarity seem like a problem rather than a benefit. What if it's undesirable for your experience in Paris to be more or less the same as your experience in Austin? Why not live like a Parisian while in Paris and a Texan while in Austin? Won't your travel experience be more authentic if you "live locally" in every city you visit and get to experience the best of what each has to offer? Framing the choice about lodging this way turns the very things that hotels are good at—standardizing experience, providing a central location for tourists, and so on—into their greatest weaknesses.

HOW TO START A MOVEMENT

You can't create a movement alone. No one can. It's your job to act as the catalyst for this next step. Just as a breakthrough idea starts with an inflection and an insight, a movement starts with a provocative story that it uses initially to enlist and motivate co-conspirators, and then ultimately uses to attract a critical mass of followers.

A provocative story defines what's at stake in the movement and energizes specific people with specific calls to action. It starts by defining a larger purpose. Consider Tesla's mission: "Accelerate the world's transition to sustainable energy." Notice that the statement doesn't even refer to the product Tesla sells. It instead defines a goal that transcends mundane concerns for products and sales. It gets people to focus on the well-being of the environment and humanity at large.

Your story must also have an enemy. That enemy is not a specific product or company. It's the status quo. Apple's 1984 commercial for the original Mac painted IBM as the "Big Brother" it was rebelling against. A couple of decades later, its "I'm a Mac and I'm a PC" ads positioned Apple against Microsoft. Salesforce campaigned against traditional enterprise software installations with its "no software" logo and slogan, contrasting incumbent weaknesses with its cloud-based approach. Although Slack didn't target a specific company, it declared "work email" as the enemy, positioning its platform as a more effective communication tool for teams. Your story must villainize the status quo by describing its problems, and by sharply contrasting between the world governed by the status quo and a world freed from its dominance. When the right people see the contrast, they need to feel an intense desire to never again accept the world as it currently is.

This is why effective language is vital to launching a movement. Breakthrough language creates demarcations in thinking, which lead to demarcations in how people feel and act. A good example is how Spotify changed the conversation around digital music. Apple's marketing campaign for its digital music device, the iPod, centered on owning songs; it used the tagline "1,000 songs in your pocket." In contrast, Spotify's language centered on renting music for a monthly fee. Spotify convinced millions of customers there was a different way to consume music. Spotify used different language to describe its different business model, with the aim of breaking the existing pattern.

Once you have a provocative story, the second step in creating a movement is to build an early coalition of the people we've referred to as co-conspirators. Your story and your call to action rally them behind a purpose that's bigger than any company or product. Building your early coalition starts with asking a simple question: Who is ready to move first?

Throughout the book, we've talked about people you'll encounter on your start-up journey: practitioners, friends, family, potential customers, and investors. Here's the thing: most are normal people, which means they expect things to stay the way they are. Many practitioners are too invested in the status quo to want to overturn it. Many people are living in the future, but they want to stay there; they aren't interested in accommodating the interests of people living in the present. Then there are the people who care about you and want the best for you. Most of them will also be normal people. As a result, they'll often react with skepticism to your new idea, albeit for well-intentioned reasons. For the founder, the temptation is to appeal to normal people because there are so many more of them. But that leads you to an incremental approach as you compromise to win them over.

Instead, it's important to recognize that there is a tiny sub-set of people you can actually move into the future, and who are prepared to move there together with you. They are your co-conspirators because they believe in your insight before others do. These are the people to focus on.

Co-conspirators are not normal people. They're zealots who steal the whiteboard pen out of your hand when you deliver a presentation to them. They're animated by belief more than utility. In prior chapters, we highlighted how start-up employees are different from normal big-company employees, how start-up customers have different motivations and risk profiles than normal customers, and how start-up investors look for different factors than traditional investors. When chosen wisely, all these individuals act as co-conspirators, joining you in a shared secret, an "us versus them" battle, uniting a passionate minority against the prevailing norms of the majority.

The canny start-up founder motivates co-conspirators by leaning into the unconventional beliefs they share—in particular, beliefs about the possibility of a different and better future. To move them forward, you need to show them that your shared beliefs about that future don't represent some abstract possibility. You need to show them that realizing that future is feasible and desirable, and you need to offer specific calls to action. The calls to action can be framed, as most great stories are, in the form of a hero's journey. It's a classic form of storytelling that we'll detail later.

I've said that your story needs to contrast the world governed by the unacceptable status quo with a possible world freed from its limits. Your story also has a hero. Your role as a founder is to make your co-conspirators heroes in their own journeys along your mutually desired path to a different future.

Here's a very important point: the hero in your story is not you. You instead play the role of mentor to your co-conspirators in their own journeys. Your task is to get them to accept your call to adventure based on your shared beliefs—to move from the world that is (the status quo) to the world that could be (the future you inhabit). In Star Wars, Obi-Wan Kenobi was the mentor and Luke Skywalker was the hero. Obi-Wan's job, like that of a start-up founder, was to persuade Luke to accept his call to adventure and fight the empire.

It's important to keep in mind that co-conspirators want something different from the normal features and benefits offered by normal companies. They are part of a conspiracy with you to realize your shared beliefs for a different future. They don't want better; they want different. When you deliver products, it's not just about features and benefits; it's about validating the beliefs of your co-conspirators in the better future they believe is possible. That means you need to force a choice and not a comparison: either inhabit the future or don't. This is why the example of the Tesla Roadster is powerful. Nobody looked at it and asked, "But how does it compare with a Porsche 911?" The Tesla Roadster did not claim to be better than the 911. It could be argued that the Roadster was worse in the ways in which cars were normally compared to each other. The Roadster couldn't be reconciled with Porsche's 911 because it offered a radically different idea of what a car could be—just as Tesla offered a radically different idea of what a car company could be.

This "us versus the rest of the world" positioning requires you to make courageous choices in the products you build. You will also embrace a different way to prioritize what matters most in making your idea a reality. If you succeed, your co-conspirators will move with you based on their belief in the aesthetically more appealing future you articulate and demonstrate. You must also give co-conspirators clear calls to action to help create a ground-swell of momentum for your beliefs to begin taking hold. It's through this process that the start-up and its co-conspirators co-create the future.

Just as it is important to find co-conspirators who believe in your insight, it is an equally important second step to avoid the temptation to be liked by normal people who still believe in the status quo. There's a constant and ongoing temptation to compromise with such people, but attempting to appeal to everyone appeals to no one. Some normal people will wish the best for you, but they will give you advice that moves you away from creating a break-through and toward acting more conventionally. Others will dismiss your idea because they won't believe in your insight, be aware of it, or care about it. Those with the biggest interest in maintaining the status quo will be actively hostile to your ideas. They will try to discredit you by whatever means they can, sometimes even using tactics that are dishonest and in bad faith. When ridesharing companies like Uber and Lyft launched, the taxi industry waged protests that blocked roads, airports, and train stations. They launched misinformation campaigns and tried to use their cozy relationships with local governments to draft burdensome regula-tions around licensing requirements, higher fees, and other rules designed to intentionally harm the business model of ridesharing. You can't let any of these things deter you by taking them person-ally. Instead, understand that it's just part of the process.

We have shown how a movement starts with the defiance of a few, and with early success it provokes the establishment to fight back. Eventually it reaches critical mass—a tipping point at which normal people go from thinking your ideas are heretical to accepting them as the new normal. Some of the most rewarding moments as a start-up investor come when I witness a company we invested in gaining mainstream recognition. I still remember the excitement when, after picking up my daughter from a play-date, her friend's mother asked if I had invested in X/Twitter. She had just seen its cofounder Evan Williams on Oprah. Similarly, when I first started seeing signs for ridesharing apps at airports alongside those for traditional rental cars and taxis, I felt a palpable sense of momentum that our ideas were winning. Now it feels like ridesharing has cemented its place in modern travel. This is what it's like when your start-up achieves the goals of the movement and establishes a new status quo, completing the sequence of radical change you set in motion. A new equilibrium sets in. Now you are the incumbent, on the lookout for the next radical start-up that's determined to overthrow your business model.

Many successful companies, once considered radical, have become such an integral part of our daily lives that it's hard to remember a time when their ideas were deemed unconventional. Just as the patterns of today are ingrained in our minds, it can be hard to remember what it was like before we embraced them. And here's a fun fact: a lot of these start-ups, after hitting it big, shift from being the cool rebels to being the main players defending their once-new rules. As a result they often become selective in recounting their initial struggles, leaving out some of the audacious and controversial steps they took in the beginning. Often they tell a new story that's more palatable to normal folks. They aim to maintain a polished, respectable image, offering a more accessible version of their origin story. That's why it's often difficult to know how the start-up days really happened.

Speaking of stories, it's time we consider another key component of creating movements: storytelling. We've hinted at its significance, and now we'll explore why stories play such a crucial role in the success of movements. That's our focus for the next chapter.

13

TELLING YOUR STORY

The Hero Isn't You

Those who tell stories rule society.
—PLATO, PHILOSOPHER, FOUNDER OF THE ACADEMY

People often think starting a movement is a matter of crafting a "message" that "resonates," or finding the right three-letter acronym or slogan. Instead, starting a movement requires crafting a story, and a story is much more than simple wordsmithing.

Humans have been moving each other with stories since their earliest days on the planet. It works because our brains are wired for stories. When you hear a powerful story, your heartbeat might increase and your body temperature may rise. It's a physical experience, and it's involuntary.

Compelling stories spread rapidly by word of mouth. This spreadability is vital to success because it accelerates the dissemination of your ideas and eliminates the need to spend money on comprehensive marketing programs—money that many start-ups don't have.

A lot of people mistakenly believe that developing a powerful story requires a type of voodoo magic. While it's true that some founders are naturally gifted at it, there are specific, concrete steps you can take to craft yours.

One key is to resist the urge to come up with taglines and acronyms, or to guess at the types of words that will "land" when you say them. Having the right words is not as important as knowing what you want to say. You start with a clear idea of what to say and how it will move people to the future you inhabit. Style matters—but only when there's substance behind it.

Above all, crafting a persuasive story for your movement involves describing your battle with the status quo and the difference between it and the new, better way that things could be. You can make your story powerful enough to inspire and motivate people. Here are the steps for doing so.

STEP 1: APPEAL TO A HIGHER PURPOSE

Political movements rally people to a cause larger than themselves. Start-up movements do the same. Tesla is now the most valuable car company. Have you seen their Super Bowl ads? Nope. They've never spent a dime on advertising—not on the Super Bowl or anywhere else. When you visit the Fremont Tesla factory to pick up a car, you see the mission statement written in letters so big they take up an entire wall of the waiting room. It bears repeating:

"Accelerate the world's transition to sustainable energy." It's not a statement about selling cars, at least not directly. They're appealing to the desire to achieve a higher purpose—a change from the world that is to a world that could be, one powered by sustainable energy.

If you're going to get people passionate about moving and passionate about convincing others to move as well, you can't just appeal to their self-interest or yours. You must appeal to their desire to achieve a purpose greater than themselves—a purpose that promises to realize a better version of who they are. They can achieve this kind of self-transformation only by doing something different from anything the status quo has to offer.

Appealing to a higher cause also helps you get marketing for free. Traditional marketing buys people's attention. Movements grounded in a powerful story get it for free as a by-product of people spreading your message for you. A story that succeeds in communicating a higher purpose motivates people to spread your ideas as an expression of their own commitment to that purpose.

STEP 2: ATTACK THE STATUS QUO

All movements make a case for change by critiquing the status quo and provoking a sense of grievance about the status quo in early believers. The status quo isn't your competitor or a specific product or a company or set of companies. Rather, it's people's established patterns of thinking, feeling, and acting—the patterns that make up the world as it currently is. Consider Tesla again. Its story attacks the use of unsustainable energy. That's the enemy, not a specific car company or alternative product offering.

The best way to attack the status quo is to reposition its greatest strengths as its greatest weaknesses. Consider Airbnb again. To create a movement away from using hotels and toward living like a local, they repositioned the standardized level of service that hotels provided—something that most normal people would think of as a strength. By focusing on this acknowledged strength, Airbnb didn't reveal anything about hotel service that people didn't already know. Their genius wasn't in revealing new facts about the service hotels offered; it was in telling a different story about that service—a story that repositioned it as a weakness instead of a strength. Airbnb realized that travelers wanted a greater sense of authenticity from their travels. The consistency of the hotel experience from location to location makes it impossible for a hotel guest to live like a local. Airbnb comprehended that travelers wanted to stay in a room that reminded them they were in Cairo, not Cleveland. As a result, it was no longer a strength that hotels could provide a room in Cairo that was indistinguishable from a room in Cleveland. On the contrary, it was a weakness.

Repositioning incumbent strengths as weaknesses is a potent opportunity, and I've found that many founders don't exploit its full potential. Start-ups often try to find gaps in other people's products—other types of weaknesses. They try to show a comparison of their features versus the incumbent's features, often in a side-by-side comparison chart where they have more boxes checked. But it's far more effective to attack an enemy based on what people already believe to be its biggest strengths. When a start-up tells a story that repositions incumbent strengths as weaknesses, it comes across as refreshingly honest.

STEP 3: CREATE A HERO'S NARRATIVE
(AND REMEMBER, THE HERO ISN'T YOU)

Your story needs to inspire in your listeners the desire to move from the world they inhabit to a new and better world that they co-create with you. Position them, you, and the status quo within the familiar narrative of the hero's journey to make clear what they should do.

In classical stories of the hero's journey, a mentor shows up and calls the hero to adventure, based initially on their mutual dissatisfaction with the world that is. The mentor offers a tool and some power or magic for using it in order to persuade the hero that the journey is possible. The hero resists. Then something bad happens to the hero. That initial setback changes the hero's mind. The hero accepts the call, uses the tool the mentor offers, taps into the magic of deeper wisdom the mentor shares, and finds new co-conspirators throughout the journey. They face trials and tribulations, defeat the bad guys and their own inner demons, and emerge victorious and different. The journey transforms them from their previous station in life to something better and more fulfilling.

In the movie *Star Wars*, the dusty and boring planet Tatooine is the world that is. Obi-Wan Kenobi is the mentor. Luke Skywalker is the hero. The lightsaber is the tool, and the Force is the power or magic to use it. Luke resists Obi-Wan's initial call to adventure to save the princess, but then his aunt and uncle are killed, and their farm is burned down by the empire. Now he's all in. Guided by Obi-Wan, Luke rescues the princess, uses the Force, blows up the Death Star, brings peace (for the moment) to the galaxy, and along the way is transformed from a mere farm boy to a Jedi warrior.

When you leverage the hero's narrative to recruit people to your movement, you need to show them the massive gap between the reigning status quo they currently must accept and what could be if they pursue the higher purpose you present. You need them to see you as a mentor offering them a new type of power or magic to use a tool that will help them succeed. And you need to tell them about the transformation they'll undergo; you need to persuade them that undertaking the journey will change them for the better—that there are important stakes involved. That's essential to a compelling story.

The people you want to persuade are on different journeys. You can't tell the very same story to each of them and expect them to appreciate the insight. The reasons a prospective employee needs to join your company are different from the reasons a prospective customer needs to buy your product. A reporter who's writing an article has a different perspective and different interests than a VC who's deciding to invest. However you tell the story, all the variations center on the same insight: your co-conspirators want to join you on a journey that leads to an adventure that will transform their lives. Don't deliver a presentation that's about you and your product and expect anyone to follow when you say, "Let's go!" They have to know why your start-up is going to help them succeed in their own hero's journey—one that's about them.

It can be tempting for founders to think of themselves as the hero. They are attracted to the hero role because our culture loves creating heroes (and tearing them down). It's a tendency reflected in the way news articles are written, and the way successful start-ups get described in hindsight. But the best entrepreneurs don't mistake themselves for the hero in their story. They realize that to move people, the story can't be about the entrepreneur. It has to be instead about the early customers, employees, and investors they're trying to inspire, and the higher purpose they're trying to get those people to embrace.

Let's return to the example of Lyft. When Logan and John presented their vision to others, they didn't position themselves as heroes. Logan and John were mentors, and they knew they needed to connect with the world that their heroes inhabited if they were going to inspire them to accept a call to adventure.

Their story had three types of heroes: riders, drivers, and investors. For riders, the world they inhabited was trying to get around San Francisco. It was a horrible experience: taxis were unreliable, and parking was nearly impossible to find. Logan and John told the riders, "You can easily request a driver with your smartphone. You'll have the power to see exactly where the driver is, and how long it will take for them to arrive."

When Logan and John talked to drivers, they told a different version of the story—one that emphasized the opportunity to make extra money working flexible hours. When they talked to investors, they told yet another version—one that emphasized the massive potential upside of the business, based on network effects.

Whatever version of the story Logan and John told, however, the story wasn't about them. They positioned their target audiences as the heroes, not themselves. If your story is going to move people, it can't be about you. It must be about the early customers, employees, and investors you're trying to inspire, and the higher purpose you want them to embrace.

Just as heroes often resist the call to adventure at first, so do your co-conspirators. In Lyft's case, John and Logan were concerned that people would be nervous about getting into a stranger's car. That's the genius of the pink mustache they attached to the fronts of the cars of the first drivers. People in San Francisco, whether in sidewalk cafes or on the streets, saw cars driving by sporting big, furry, pink mustaches. It caused people to talk about the cars and tell others about the new service, and it led them to give the service the benefit of the doubt.

It's good to anticipate why your early co-conspirators might resist your call to adventure and to find a way to make it easier for them to accept that call.

STEP 4: FORCE A CHOICE, NOT A COMPARISON

Christopher Lochhead, the self-described "dogfather of category design," is a notable figure with a vivid backstory. Hailing from Montreal, Canada, Lochhead attributes the moniker "dogfather" to being dyslexic, which led to his dropping out of high school. Unable to secure a conventional job, he started a company in the computer training sector. The venture was tough at first but paved the way for his illustrious career in Silicon Valley.

For Lochhead, dyslexia wasn't a setback; rather, it afforded a different perspective that helped him approach business and marketing innovatively. After holding key marketing positions in several public companies, he coauthored the bestseller *Play Bigger*. This book introduced the idea of category design, which is a business strategy framework that emphasizes creating and dominating a new market category rather than competing within an existing one. It's about defining, developing, and evangelizing a new market space where your solution or product is not just a better option but the only option.

Category design offers a worldview that's crucial for founders with pattern-breaking ambitions. The idea is to force a choice, not a comparison.

When the iPhone was introduced in 2007, Steve Jobs didn't just present it as a better phone. He described a reinvention of the phone, which combined a "revolutionary mobile phone," a "widescreen iPod with touch controls," and a "breakthrough Internet communicator." It wasn't positioned merely as an improvement on existing phones but as a unique product category of its own. After the iPhone launch, people didn't ask, "But how is that different from a Blackberry?"

Instead of positioning their cars as better versions of existing luxury vehicles, Tesla focused on creating a new category of luxury car that escaped comparison with traditional gas-powered luxury cars. When people saw a Tesla, they didn't ask, "But how is that different from a BMW?"

When Uber and Lyft rolled onto the scene, they didn't pitch themselves as a fresher version of a yellow cab. They offered the novel concept "Push a button, get a ride." It was so distinct that those wandering the streets of San Francisco seeking transportation didn't find themselves asking, "But how is that different from taxis?" Instead, they readily joined the transportation revolution happening right before their eyes.

Founders fall into a comparison trap whenever they compete on features or price or any aspect of "betterness," such as:

Faster (than what?)

Smarter (than what?)

More economical (than what?)

Most efficient (compared to what?)

Why is it a bad idea for pattern-breaking start-ups to tell stories this way?

The distinction is nuanced yet crucial: when you frame your story around being "better," you inadvertently accept the existing standard set by established players. This tacitly concedes that the prevailing model defined by the status quo remains relevant. In doing so, you forfeit the opportunity to redefine the game on your terms, without fully realizing what you've given up.

Breakthrough founders tell a story about a different future, not a better present. They force a choice ("Here's the different future we can create together") rather than a comparison ("I'm faster, smarter, cheaper"). The latter defines your start-up relative to the status quo.

Consider a couple of famous breakthroughs. When Thomas Edison successfully demonstrated the first long-lasting incandescent light bulb in 1879, people did not ask, "How is this better than whale oil lamps or beeswax candles?" It was a radically different way to produce light that had no comparison. They wanted to know how quickly it could be wired into their homes.

When the Wright brothers showed that human flight was possible, people didn't ask, "But how does that compare with trains?" It was the dawn of a new category of transportation.

Edison and the Wright brothers are vivid illustrations of how pattern breakers refuse to buy into the premise of the current rules. That's what it means to force a choice and not a comparison.

What's so bad about playing the comparison game if you're better? No matter how good you get, if you play the comparison game, you can't change the rules—because you're playing by the rules the incumbents set. If you can't change the rules, you have limited upside. You can't radically change how people live. You can't wage an unfair fight that's biased to your difference. By forcing a choice, not a comparison, breakthroughs define their own rules, and that creates the potential for far greater upside.

We're bombarded with comparison messages, all vying for our money and attention. As you drive down the road, you see the three-point star on the hood of the Mercedes coming your way. When you walk into a supermarket, you see the logos of the companies behind every product on the shelves. When you choose your morning coffee, you are likely loyal to a certain brand. It never stops. It's a stream of marketing messages that are either trying to get you to change the ways you go about the world, or trying to get you to double down on the ways you already do.

This bombardment has become so commonplace that we've learned to tune it out. People automatically categorize products and ideas in what amounts to containers in their heads. Coca-Cola? That goes in the soft drink container in my mind. So does Pepsi. Mercedes? Park over there in the luxury car container next to the Lexus.

These containers reduce the cognitive load of getting through each day, and they shape how all of us live our lives. If I'm the CFO of a company with a line-item budget and someone proposes a budget for a new thing, the first thing I am likely to ask is "What part of my budget (i.e., category) does that come out of?" As a consumer considering a new smartphone purchase, I might ask what fraction of my monthly budget I should spend and what part of my budget it will come from. If I visit my friend Christopher Lochhead in his hometown of Santa Cruz, California, and he says, "Let's go to the Alderwood restaurant for dinner," the odds are quite high that my next question will be, "What kind of restaurant is Alderwood?" What's important is the way we put things in containers to make sense of them and see where they fit in the patterns of our understanding of the world.

A start-up wins when it breaks the pattern and introduces a fresh concept that reshapes people's perceptions and sets its own standards. However, if the concept merely fits into an existing container, it often faces stiff competition and must abide by pre-established rules set by incumbents. In such a situation, the start-up will be compared to existing players, making it harder to stand out. By contrast, when a product or service creates a new container in someone's mind, it escapes the comparison trap and lets the innovator define the rules. Steve Jobs excelled at defining new containers during his later years at Apple. He showed how this approach can also be used by bigger companies seeking to break patterns of existing capabilities and competitive rules. Instead of simply improving on existing MP3 players, he reimagined them with the iPod, promoting the groundbreaking idea of "1,000 songs in your pocket" and introducing the intuitive click wheel and the transformative iTunes platform. With the iPhone, he reshaped expectations of what a phone should be. Apple shifted the power from carriers like AT&T and Verizon, which traditionally controlled phone features, to Apple and, later, other device manufacturers. Similarly, the iPad wasn't just another laptop; it established tablets as a distinct category in computing. In each of these cases, competitors soon found themselves aligning with Apple's vision, effectively operating by Apple's rules within the containers Apple had created.

Inviting a comparison is a trap because the terms of the comparison are defined by the incumbent that originally established the container. When you live in someone else's container, you play by their rules. It's not credible for a start-up to say, "Look at me. I have a better version of what they have. Pay no attention to the fact that we have hardly any money, people, or proof points." What's better eventually fades into the noise of what is. The only way for a start-up to cut through that noise is by being different enough to create its own category.

STEP 5: FIND YOUR BREAKTHROUGH LANGUAGE

Breakthrough start-ups need a breakthrough language to match their breakthrough product. Lyft didn't talk about a taxi app; it instead talked about ridesharing—a new container. If Lyft had described itself as a taxi service, it would have invited comparison with other taxi services.

Christopher Lochhead calls the task of crafting the right words for the job "languaging." "Languaging" is a verb because it catalyzes new actions in real people. Differences in language create differences in thought, and different thoughts lead real people in the real world to feel and act differently. Languaging affects every aspect of the way people think about your movement versus the status quo. This includes your product's features, the higher purpose you promote, and the choice you force.

One indication that your languaging needs more work is when people ask you to add features to your product that incumbents' products have. One of two things is then true: either you haven't forced a choice—a new container that people can get excited about—or else you aren't talking to the right people. If the former, you need to develop a new language that emphasizes your difference. If the latter, you need to find the right potential co-conspirators to talk with, a topic we explored in Chapters 10 and 11.

When discussing ideas with potential collaborators, be wary of confirmation bias. There's a natural inclination to focus on positive feedback that validates our beliefs and to downplay negative or opposing views. It's easy to sidestep challenging questions that test our assumptions or to seek opinions primarily from our close circle, like friends or family. However, the goal isn't to gather feedback from those who simply like us; it's crucial to engage in meaningful conversations with the rare individuals who potentially share our vision and insights.

STORYTELLING TAKEAWAYS

Great movements start with powerful stories. By crafting a powerful story, founders inspire people to join them and move to the future they inhabit.

1. Define a higher purpose that rallies people to a cause bigger than themselves and your company.

2. Describe what's wrong with the status quo. Draw a clear contrast between the status quo and a future committed to the higher purpose you're promoting.

3. Create a compelling narrative that makes the person you wish to persuade the hero in their own hero's journey. You do this by contrasting their chances of completing the journey if things stay as they are with their chances of completing it if they move with you to a new and different future. You give them confidence that they'll succeed by positioning yourself as a mentor and sharing with them your insight and idea. You also anticipate why they might resist your call to adventure, and you meet this resistance.

4. Force a choice and not a comparison. You need to be different, not merely better.

5. Resist the temptation to use language that already exists in the market. Use new language that leads to new ways of thinking.

Although creating a movement begins with telling a compelling story, it doesn't end there. Most people aren't ready to move yet, no matter what you say.

14

BE DISAGREEABLE

And Not a Jerk

The opposite of courage in our society is not cowardice; it is conformity.

—ROLLO MAY, AMERICAN PSYCHOLOGIST AND AUTHOR

The word "disagreeable" reminds me of a Rorschach test, where people examine inkblots and project their own interpretations. For some, disagreeableness is a social defect. It conjures up the image of the boorish party guest or the curmudgeonly relative who ruins family gatherings. A more ominous perspective involves manipulation, animosity toward others, or even outright cruelty, deception, or fraud. Others regard disagreeableness as a sign of resisting conformity and staying authentic, demonstrated by a person's willingness to voice unfiltered opinions, establish distinct boundaries, refuse to lower their standards, and directly address conflict.

I'm describing disagreeableness in the context of the "big five" personality traits often discussed in the fields of psychology and neuroscience. These attributes include openness to new experiences, conscientiousness, extraversion, agreeableness, and neuroticism. This model, often abbreviated as OCEAN, is a widely recognized method for understanding individual personalities.

According to the OCEAN model, individuals who are high in the agreeableness personality trait are generally warm, friendly, and tactful. Those who are low in agreeableness are considered disagreeable. They often display skepticism, competitiveness, bluntness, low empathy, low concern for social harmony, and more independence in thinking and behavior.

AGREE TO BE DISAGREEABLE

As I reflect on the characteristics of founders who create pattern-breaking start-ups, I have observed that the right amount of disagreeableness can be a founder's ally in developing breakthrough ideas and forming the movements that make them real. This notion of disagreeableness as a positive trait isn't front and center in academic journals or mainstream business articles. It is something that is important but not fully explored. As we understand how to increase the chances of a breakthrough, I wish to highlight a few specific advantages of disagreeableness that I have noticed.

Disagreeableness enables non-consensus ideas and actions, breakthrough ideas that are right even when others think they're wrong. This trait goes beyond coming up with pattern-breaking ideas. It includes the courage to act outside the norm. Consider the unorthodox founders behind Justin.tv. Recall that they auctioned off their first start-up, Kiko, on eBay. Yes, eBay, the marketplace for used guitars and vintage clothing, became their stage for selling a tech start-up. Or recall how Airbnb, in its earliest days, funded itself through the most untraditional means: by selling $40 cereal boxes adorned with the faces of Barack Obama and John McCain during the presidential election of 2008. (The boxes had cost them $4 each to make.) These were actions that, by any standard business playbook, would seem risky if not completely bizarre. In both cases, they succeeded!

Justin and Emmett selling Kiko for $258,000 was a huge outcome for two guys barely out of college with a doomed start-up. The sale was also a tangible demonstration of how the founders could use a conventional auction system in an unconventional way. For Airbnb, the "Obama O's" and "Cap'n McCain's" cereal boxes helped them get noticed and receive funding from famed start-up accelerator Y Combinator. At the end of their interview, Airbnb's cofounders showed Y Combinator founders Paul Graham and Jessica Livingston the boxes of cereal. After they had described how they'd made $30,000 by selling them, a bemused Paul Graham said, "If you can convince people to pay $40 for a $4 box of cereal, maybe you can get strangers to stay in other strangers' homes."

GETTING TO "NO"

Disagreeableness knows when to say no. Two seductive myths are often emphasized in normal business: the customer is always right, and harmony within the team is desirable. We have found that it's often the willingness to say no for the right reasons that protects pattern-breaking ideas from the forces that can dilute their power to catalyze radical change. Some of Okta's early prospective customers wanted Okta to integrate its innovative cloud identity-management capabilities with legacy applications. Adding this type of feature enhancement would have been the agreeable, easy route. The founders of Okta could easily have said yes, kept the peace, and made the sale to those customers.

But the Okta founders were disagreeable to this request (and others)—and for the right reasons. They realized that not every early prospective customer was the right customer. They saw that saying yes to the wrong features for the wrong customer could be an agreement they would later regret. Their resistance was not stubbornness; it was clarity of mission. They were keeping their product as a pure play: Okta handled only cloud identity-management applications. They chose customers who shared their view of the future over those who might provide short-term revenue but long-term regret.

Todd and Freddy of Okta had the courage to be disagreeable when it came to prioritizing the right product capabilities for the right target customers. In a world that often rewards compromise, truly transformative founders take the uncomfortable step of holding their ground on their vision, even when it's easier to just say yes. It's tempting to latch on to any form of validation, but this is when founders must be most vigilant. Todd and Freddy were pattern-breaking founders who were able to discern between customers who were truly on board with their pioneering vision and those who would derail it with well-intentioned but ultimately misguided demands. They were not being inflexible or ignoring advice just to prove they were right. They listened to the suggestions that aligned with their vision while pushing back on those that would compromise it.

Directness and integrity apply across the board to everyone you decide to enlist in your movement. Whether it's with initial customers, the start-up team, investors, or other early believers, it's usually better to be straightforward to the point of bluntness than it is to be concerned about offending people by being honest.

REJECTING REJECTION

Disagreeableness counters negativity and rejection. Start-ups that achieve greatness often experience constant early rejection. When Dropbox founder Drew Houston initially posted a video demo of Dropbox on a popular site called Hacker News, he received many negative comments. They are entertaining to read in hindsight, but they tested Drew's confidence in his idea. One critic remarked, "For a Linux user, you can already build such a system for yourself quite trivially." Another suggested, "You still need to carry a USB drive in case there are connectivity problems." Another doubter opined, "Does not seem very 'viral' or income-generating." Investor feedback mirrored these sentiments: "Google is going to do this." "Online storage is a commodity." "This looks like a feature, not a company." As Drew points out, if you're doing something interesting and new, criticism and rejection are a rite of passage. His guidance to fellow dreamers and founders: "You simultaneously must have thick skin and be able to tune negativity like that out. But you also must have thin skin if your customers or team aren't happy and respond to it. . . . It's a weird dynamic that you're going to have to handle, but I think it starts with getting some perspective that you will always face negativity and criticism from some people."

This resilience is crucial, requiring an intrinsic confidence that doesn't waver in the face of naysayers but is fueled by an unwavering belief in your own vision.

WATCH OUT! IT'S A TRAP

Disagreeableness defends against the conformity trap. In the world of start-ups, there's an underlying tension between social harmony and the relentless pursuit of the mission. The air is thick with your ambition, but your resources are thin. Here, the gravitational pull mustn't be toward consensus or garnering approval from others, but toward mission clarity and rapid execution. It's not about neglecting the human dimension; rather, it's about elevating the objectives surrounding your mission to a revered status.

In every project we undertake, the pressures to conform to the expectations of others are immense. From early childhood, societal norms and expectations shape our behavior, values, and identity. Family members are often the first to impose conformity, passing on traditions, beliefs, and expectations. Schools exert pressure by setting behavioral standards and promoting competition. Peers influence conformity through the need to fit in. Media plays a significant role by broadcasting societal norms that influence self-perception and behavior.

From a biological perspective, we are hardwired to chase approval of our peers. By being more agreeable and fitting in, we promote harmony and reduce conflict. We're less likely to feel the sting of rejection. And it takes less cognitive effort to go with the flow. Without our consciously realizing it, our internal voices constantly pressure us to conform when we doubt our ideas and abilities or worry about how we will be judged by others.

In other words, just as the lack of a fundamental insight about the future can lead a start-up unwittingly into a *comparison* trap, the embedded tendency of people to adhere to the expectations of the status quo can lead a start-up unwittingly into a conformity trap. The *conformity* trap lures you into aligning with societal expectations, orthodox behaviors, and traditional paths to the detriment of pursuing a divergent path you believe is better. By entrapping yourself this way, you forfeit your chance to become the pattern breaker you aspire to be.

It's like being a whistleblower who's too polite to blow the whistle. Imagine if Lyft had asked for permission from the San Francisco government to launch its ridesharing service. The answer would have certainly been no. Lyft understood that to ask permission was to seek denial. Their only feasible route to acceptance was through customers' delight in their service, which paved the way for meaningful dialogues with local authorities. To succeed at fulfilling their mission, Lyft's founders had to avoid what would have been a lethal conformity trap of requesting permission to innovate.

CONFRONTATION, NOT CONGENIALITY

Many of us are trained to have a very tidy picture of what a good business leader looks like: Be slow to criticize, and be generous with praise in public. Don't shout. Seek harmony and find common ground. Stress agreement over disagreement.

Yet the most transformative leaders—the ones who reframe the paradigms of industries—often stir the pot instead of calming the waters.

Consider the tale of a young Bill Gates at Microsoft. Here's a man who fostered a culture not of congeniality but of confrontation. He made it his mission to probe, prod, and provoke questions that were often antagonistic. Meetings were intellectual battlegrounds where he relentlessly pressed people. He had little patience for ambiguity or lack of preparation. But his emotional interrogations weren't just about creating tension for tension's sake. Rather, they were a reflection of Gates's commitment to extraordinarily high standards.

The impact of Bill's confrontational ethos? In my observation, it turned out to be oddly motivating. That is the paradox of confrontational leadership. It doesn't just identify the weak links; it forges stronger ones. So although much of the mainstream business world praises agreeable leaders, I say let's hear it for the ones who aren't afraid to make us uncomfortable. Because sometimes, that's exactly what we need to be our best selves.

I've heard many other examples of leaders who have been tough on people when it came to their expectations. The world of pattern-breaking founders is flush with these confrontational figures—people like Steve Jobs, Elon Musk, Jeff Bezos, and others—who don't exactly adhere to the *How to Win Friends and Influence People* playbook. Could it be that those who are willing to bring the hottest heat of expectations are the ones who forge the strongest alloys? Perhaps the most potent motivation for the most committed and talented is not the prospect of agreement but the reality of challenge. In a world where we're often encouraged to avoid unpleasant conversations, it's worth remembering that sometimes, to break a pattern, we need leaders who expect and require the same level of performance from others as they expect from themselves. They demand the best from their team and from themselves in the pursuit of greatness.

Many other disagreeable tendencies contribute to a higher likelihood of pattern-breaking success, including the willingness to aggressively push your negotiating position and the tendency to seek ways to redefine the rules rather than comply with them. But my aim isn't to list every single aspect of disagreeableness that makes it a powerful factor in achieving extraordinary success. My goal is simpler. I want to show you how this trait is crucial in driving people to achieve life-changing accomplishments.

FINDING YOUR BALANCE

What does this mean for founders looking to challenge the status quo? Instead of shaping a new identity, one that is either more or less disagreeable, it is better to gain a deeper understanding of your current self.

Many people have learned to be overly agreeable because of societal expectations and a desire for approval. But in the quest for approval, lots of people veer into the realm of inauthenticity. The irony is that you're told to be yourself, but then you're also told to dilute your convictions, to temper your questions, to sugarcoat your criticisms—all in the name of keeping everyone around you comfortable. And here's what we ought to realize: this form of agreeableness—this constant yielding to the comfort zones of others—is not a hallmark of true empathy or compassion. It's a mask we wear in the theater of social interaction. In doing so, we sacrifice not just our mission, whatever it might be, but something even more fundamental: our very sense of self, our authentic being. When you mute your skepticism, when you gloss over your genuine feedback, when you compromise your core beliefs, you are negotiating away your integrity. And what you're left with is not a more agreeable you, but a less authentic you—a you that's out of sync with your true mission and potential.

And yet at the other extreme, we encounter some who have found a convenient sanctuary in the narrative of disagreeableness. They are the wrecking balls, the sledgehammers that demolish dignity and respect in the name of "authenticity." They label their behavior "disagreeable" as though that term were a cloak of courage, a get-out-of-jail-free card for conduct that crosses the line from challenging to damaging, from confrontational to cruel. And here's the frustrating paradox: some of these people succeed in their pattern-breaking ambitions, providing an intoxicating model that others seek to imitate.

But in most cases, these individuals haven't triumphed because of their abrasive demeanor; they've succeeded despite it. Their skills, brilliance, and originality have effectively served as a counterweight to their obnoxiousness. The misunderstanding lies in mistaking corrosiveness for courage, rudeness for resolve. Being obnoxious isn't an audacious act of authenticity; it's a smoke screen, a way to sidestep facing one's internal insecurities. It's not an affirmation of one's true self but rather a deviation from a more mature understanding of genuine authenticity.

And then there is the biggest cautionary tale of them all: the fraudulent pseudovisionary. This individual projects the aura and charisma often associated with someone authentically committed to groundbreaking missions, effectively masquerading as the kind of disagreeable leader we instinctively trust to bring about meaningful change. But here lies the trap. These impostors manipulate our tendency to place faith in audacious innovators, not for the pursuit of a great purpose but to perpetrate fraud. They weaponize our admiration for courageous leadership to serve a deceptive agenda, offering us a master class in the hazards of misplaced trust.

Perhaps the most infamous case from recent years is Elizabeth Holmes of Theranos, who promised to revolutionize the medical-testing industry. Using her charisma and storytelling skills, she was able to attract high-profile board members and significant investment. However, it later emerged in court testimony that the technology she touted did not work as promised. She was convicted of massive fraud and is now serving time in prison. Billy McFarland promoted the luxurious Fyre Festival using social media and influencer marketing. The event was considered a total disaster, and McFarland pleaded guilty to fraud and was sentenced to years in prison.

The line between unconventional brilliance and fraud can sometimes appear blurry, especially in fast-moving industries like technology. Charisma and public attention can sometimes mask serious ethical and legal shortcomings. Many of the stress tests we've described in prior chapters provide a rigorously objective lens, allowing us to differentiate enterprises that are built to change the future from those that are built to exploit the gullible.

Assuming you're committed to achieving genuine break-throughs, and not mere illusions, the question you must confront is "How can I elevate myself to be my most authentic, best self?" To do this, I advocate securing a top-tier executive coach from day one of your entrepreneurial journey. It's far better to do this at the out-set, before your organization becomes dysfunctional and in need of repair. Most of us are not the fully realized versions of ourselves we aspire to be. Yet with the assistance of a seasoned guide, you can chart a course toward your envisioned self. If your natural disposi-tion leans toward agreeableness and pulls you in the direction of the conformity trap, your executive coach serves as the crucial counter-balance. He or she guides you toward a brand of disagreeableness that isn't just authentic, but strategically advantageous, orienting you toward your mission rather than social appeasement. Con-versely, if your demeanor is innately challenging, edging occasion-ally toward the destructive or even the obnoxious, a skilled coach helps you channel that disagreeableness more constructively, with-out alienating those critical to your mission's success.

The common denominator, irrespective of your starting posi-tion, is insightful, brutally honest feedback that you can trust. An adept executive coach is more than just a consultant; they're a mirror reflecting both your brilliance and your blind spots. And in the push to achieve greatness, understanding and acting on those blind spots isn't just helpful. It's nonnegotiable.

DISAGREEABLENESS TAKEAWAYS
The business arena is never a level playing field. The scales nat-urally tip toward incumbents, favoring their established norms.

Agreeableness, for all its social graces, seldom shatters molds or changes the future. Breaking patterns calls for a bit of disagreeableness.

1. Excessive agreeableness is not authentic. If your ambition is to recast the future, those who fiercely cling to the status quo might exploit your innate desire for acceptance, pressuring you to act against your core convictions. Agreeing for the sake of getting along with others, when it goes against your internal beliefs, is another form of insincerity. Your movement begins with a cohort of true believers that must triumph against a sizable majority. Therefore, you must summon the courage and develop the temperament to doggedly chase your insights, often confronting outright hostility to your movement. It's crucial to avoid the conformity trap, and agreeableness risks undermining your mission. This principle rings true in all your interactions, be they with skeptics, advisers, team members, investors, regulatory authorities, or any other party whose interests could positively or negatively influence your start-up's mission. Any true movement stirs a minority to stand against the majority. Seeking the approval of an indifferent or even antagonistic majority can dilute the potency of your message and its ability to draw in the potential early believers you care most about. It's this kind of courage, this refusal to capitulate to the status quo, that fuels the spirit of early believers.

2. Excessive disagreeableness is not authentic either. Authenticity, at its core, involves a balance between standing by your principles and being open to new ideas or viewpoints that can strengthen your understanding of how to fuel your direction forward. Constant disagreement, being contrarian for its own sake, is a type of conformity that reacts against the thinking of other people. It is different from genuine disagreement based on deeply held beliefs or convictions. It's vital to both uphold your values and principles and guard against overvaluing a contentiousness that impedes you and your team. Ultimately, you cannot make a movement successful on your own. You need the collective efforts of others who share your vision. Gratuitous or excessive confrontation can push away these early supporters, the ones your movement relies on the most. Therefore, any disagreeable behavior that hinders the shared effort becomes counterproductive to accomplishing your mission.

3. Disagreeableness buys freedom. Perseverance and conviction keep your non-consensus idea whole and inspire others to join your movement. The more you seek approval from others, the less free you will be to pursue the remarkable. You need to decide which master to serve most faithfully—the mission you want to make your life's work, or the approval of others with an agenda different from yours.

4. Find the courage to accept and be your best self. Every founder has both flaws and strengths; the challenge is for you to see them in their true light. Don't lie to your-

self by letting self-deceptive beliefs obscure uncomfort-able truths that can hold you back from doing some-thing great.

5. The more disagreeable you are, the lonelier your exis-tence. Disagreeableness can be a spark that ignites rev-olutions. Yet that same spark often burns bridges that connect us to community and friendship. The very qualities that drive groundbreaking change are the same ones that can sentence us to a form of social and emo-tional isolation. As you build your breakthrough, you will alienate others and occasionally feel alienated from yourself when you experience the pain of self-doubt. This is where the benefit of having cofounders comes into play, especially those who can get along despite their disagreeableness.

15

DANCING ELEPHANTS

How Corporations Can Be Pattern Breakers

When elephants dance, the grass gets trampled.
—AFRICAN PROVERB

Can elephants dance to the different beat of a pattern-breaking rhythm?

We believe the answer is yes. Large corporations can harness inflection theory to wage offensive battles. But an asterisk looms large: transformational innovation is no small feat, especially for well-run businesses.

THE BIASES OF SUCCESS
People often oversimplify the challenges large corporations face when trying to develop pattern-breaking new products and lines

of business. Surface-level explanations include complacency, aversion to risk, market shortsightedness, bureaucratic bottlenecks, or even cultural stagnation. But these reasons often miss the deeper dynamics. The real challenge may not be overcoming a lack of drive, but relying on the patterns of operating that have led to past successes. Frequently it's not complacency that hampers radical innovation; it's the bias of existing success.

Why is that?

The accumulation of experiences from past successes encourages corporations to build on what works. But it also encourages adherence to preestablished patterns, precisely due to their reliable contribution to consistent and compounding bottom-line success. Unfortunately, the patterns create biases that hinder fresh and innovative perspectives.

By contrast, pattern-breaking start-ups don't generate value by compounding their core business—they do not have a business yet! Their very existence centers on creating radical, game-changing inventions.

This is a key reason that pattern-breaking innovations, even in established markets, often come from outsiders rather than insiders. Ridesharing wasn't the brainchild of Hertz or Avis. It came from Uber and Lyft. The short-term housing-rental concept didn't spring from Hilton but from Airbnb. Boeing and Lockheed didn't commercialize many of the innovative concepts that SpaceX successfully brought to market. GM and Toyota achieved modest success in electric vehicles before Tesla showed what a radically different approach could look like. Well-known venture capitalist Vinod Khosla describes these examples of "noninstitutional reinvention" as the predominant way new breakthroughs happen.

A corporation's success can introduce several different types of bias against achieving breakthroughs.

A bias toward existing value creation: Established businesses build value by focusing on their core operations. They optimize and leverage existing advantages to deter new entrants and dominate competitors. In contrast, breakthrough businesses seek radically new opportunities and transformative changes. They aim to rewrite the rules of the game, focusing on discovering entirely new ways of creating value.

A bias against risk-taking: Established businesses equate risk with uncertainty and aim to avoid it, following Warren Buffett's cautionary advice. Breakthrough builders, however, view uncertainty as an inherent part of innovation. They embrace calculated risk-taking as an essential part of the journey to success since great upside is often found in the unexplored.

A bias toward punishing failure: In established businesses, executives often shy away from risky projects due to the career-threatening nature of failure. This cautious approach comes with its own invisible price tag. In sidestepping the risk of near-term failure, established organizations unwittingly place themselves on the trajectory for a different type of failure: the inability to achieve new breakthroughs. When we gravitate toward opportunities that carry a low risk of failure, we inadvertently eliminate a whole universe of breakthrough opportunities. As Vinod Khosla puts it, such companies reduce the risk of failure so much that "the consequences of success are inconsequential." Corporations not only minimize the chance of failure; they also minimize the chance of a breakthrough. In contrast, pattern breakers are willing to risk initial failures for the chance to pursue breakthrough opportunities. They measure risk by expected value—which is the probability of success multiplied by the value of success—rather than by the avoidance of failure.

A bias toward agreeableness: In established businesses, leaders prioritize stability and alignment, traits that are rewarded with career advancement. Their focus is on disciplined execution within existing frameworks. Breakthrough builders, however, are akin to rebellious pirates who thrive on defying norms and envisioning alternative futures. The skills that make someone a successful manager in a traditional setting often clash with the disruptive tendencies needed for breakthrough innovations. This mismatch often leads to dissatisfaction, especially for start-up founders who find themselves feeling trapped in large companies after their start-up is acquired. Not surprisingly, these founders frequently depart at the earliest opportunity.

A bias against new approaches: Auto executives once derided the poor quality of Tesla's cars compared with the craftsmanship of a Mercedes or the elegance of an Audi. Other experts said Tesla would fail because the company didn't have a background in large-scale automotive manufacturing. Tesla's control over its entire supply chain, including owning its stores and service centers, was a break from traditional industry practice; many considered it unworkable. What they missed is that Tesla wasn't just building a car; Tesla was redefining the rules of the auto industry in every aspect, from manufacturing to product design to distribution to the very definition of what a car should be in the first place.

A bias toward corporate metrics: Established businesses rely on traditional financial metrics like return on net assets, earnings per share, return on invested capital, and internal rate of return to guide funding and measure success. Start-ups, lacking such metrics, must stress-test whether they are harnessing inflections and insights that can spark radical change.

Other pressures faced by big companies reduce their likelihood to break patterns: The demands of their existing customer base. The pressure to achieve quarterly performance targets. The challenge of having people who excel at making the business run smoothly, but who wouldn't know where to start if the goal were to create a radically different business.

Can these finely tuned corporate engines have the best of both worlds? Can they dominate existing businesses and radically change the way people think, feel, and act?

We believe the answer is yes. But the journey is far from simple.

BREAKING FREE FROM INCREMENTALISM

Breaking free from incremental success is a long shot. That said, compelling outliers do exist, big companies that somehow found a way to maintain their status as incumbents and still break the mold. These companies either capitalized on organic innovation, building something groundbreaking from square one; or they acquired other companies that were already breaking patterns; or they formed bold partnerships, joining forces with other entities to explore new frontiers. Let's look at examples of each of these strategies.

Organic Innovation

Recently celebrated examples of organic innovation often focus on technology companies like Apple with the iPhone or Amazon with Amazon Web Services. These pattern-breaking examples, while compelling, seem less relevant to corporate leaders whose businesses are not technology-centric. Fortunately, enduring examples exist elsewhere.

In 1943, the US War Department hired Lockheed Aircraft Corporation to secretly develop a high-speed fighter jet within 180 days. They specified that it have a top speed of six hundred miles per hour, more than two hundred mph faster than Lockheed's existing P-38 propeller plane, the Lightning. Operating under tight constraints, including limited office space and a shoestring budget, Lockheed entrusted the task to chief engineer Clarence "Kelly" Johnson. This project gave birth to Skunk Works, Lockheed's lab for top-secret and innovative programs.

Johnson, along with twenty-three handpicked designers and engineers and thirty mechanics, broke away from Lockheed's main operations, setting up in a rented circus tent next to a foul-smelling plastics factory. The nickname "Skunk Works" evolved from a comic strip reference and eventually became the official alias of Lockheed Advanced Development Programs.

Skunk Works is associated with efficient, secretive, and rapid business practices. The group's ability to innovate and deliver products ahead of schedule was demonstrated by its creation of the XP-80 jet fighter (Lulu Belle) in just 143 days. While the XP-80 didn't see action in World War II, its timely delivery set the stage for the dominance of America's front-line fighter jets in the Korean War.

Kelly's approach to innovation is encapsulated in fourteen rules, which are proudly displayed on Lockheed Martin's website. Several of them apply only to military projects, but the following eight principles, paraphrased here, are powerful for any team wishing to build a breakthrough.

1. Appoint one master of all. Designate a project leader with full control, and have them report only to a division president or higher.

2. Viciously minimize the team. Restrict the team's size to enhance productivity. The selection should be based on talent and the ability to move quickly.

3. Locate somewhere small. Find a small yet well-equipped facility to reinforce the strong and productive team dynamics.

4. Stay away from outsiders. Keep the project under wraps to prevent executive interference and delays. Even if your product is not top secret, let your team fly under the radar, unconstrained by potential meddling from higher-ups. This way you will not deal with unwanted delays or the problems introduced by making a project too visible before enough is known about the likelihood of success or the path to success.

5. Document your work, but not every step. Minimize reports, but record essential work and have frequent cost reviews.

6. Deliver early and continuously. Enable the team to iterate easily, focusing on producing tangible deliverables early and regularly.

7. Involve the whole team in the big picture. People get more creative when they understand the larger picture beyond just their role.

8. Reward performance, not status. Less concern about supervisory levels and direct reports reinforces the goal of lean execution.

Kelly and the Skunk Works example is a great illustration of how building breakthroughs is a fundamentally different endeavor from optimizing core businesses in various ways, including value creation, risk profile, required talent, and success measurement. Recognizing this disparity, Kelly succeeded by creating a lean, autonomous group that could operate separately from the core business at its earliest stages.

Mergers and Acquisitions

Mergers and acquisitions also present pattern-breaking opportunities. Some mergers are most suitable for enhancing the core business. In these cases, the target company's assets and market position can be seamlessly integrated into the existing business model. Such opportunities should align with the risk profile of the core business, carrying a higher likelihood of success, and should leverage the current business model rather than attempting to reinvent it. A prime example is Apple's acquisition of P.A. Semiconductor, which enabled the integration of talent and technology into Apple's existing device ecosystem.

Other mergers are better suited for accelerating breakthrough opportunities that reimagine the business model. Like breakthrough organic innovations, these mergers are most effective when targeting high-risk ventures with asymmetrical returns. A notable illustration of a successful breakthrough acquisition is the information-management company EMC Corporation's acquisition of VMware, which enabled EMC's customers to explore entirely new virtual-server environments, an area where EMC had not traditionally played a leadership role.

The mistake many companies make is failing to recognize that the principles governing organic business breakthroughs are equally applicable to mergers and acquisitions. The risk profile, the individuals involved, the anticipated upside, and the impact on extending or reinventing the business model are just as crucial for acquired properties as they are for organically developed initiatives.

Combining the best of both worlds provides the mode for success: the assets possessed by the core business plus the new inflections and insights harnessed by the acquisition target. Facebook's acquisition of Instagram is a good example. In 2012, Facebook's mobile penetration was quite low, and the mobile app Instagram was taking off like a rocket. When Mark Zuckerberg acquired Instagram for $1 billion, most people thought he overpaid. But Facebook combined its distribution engine with the freshness of Instagram's mobile capabilities. Zuckerberg also let Instagram's cofounder Kevin Systrom run Instagram autonomously for quite some time while giving Systrom access to Facebook's assets when he thought he could leverage them for Instagram's benefit. Today Instagram has billions of users and generated over $43 billion in 2022 revenues.

These examples and others—such as Disney's acquisition of Pixar, Procter & Gamble's acquisition of Gillette, and Google's acquisition of YouTube—show that bold acquisitions can enable parent companies to change the rules and go beyond making mere incremental gains in their existing lines of business.

Partnerships

Audacious partnerships offer another route to pattern breaking. United Airlines' 2021 partnership with Boom Supersonic is an intriguing case study. Boom, founded by Blake Scholl, a former software engineer and aviation enthusiast, is designing a new generation of commercial supersonic airplanes. In collaboration with United Airlines, Boom hopes to revolutionize the airline industry, which has seen little real innovation in decades.

Supersonic commercial flight, though a reality in the past with the Concorde, faced insurmountable economic and environmental challenges due to low fuel efficiency and limited passenger capacity. Boom aims to change that narrative with its Overture airliner, which is capable of flying at speeds of Mach 1.7. This new aircraft could nearly halve the time required for trans-Atlantic flights, turning a journey from New York to London into a three-and-a-half-hour flight. United Airlines has committed to buying fifteen Overtures, with an option for thirty-five more provided Boom meets certain requirements.

United's CEO, Scott Kirby, made a daring decision to forge this partnership, fully aware of the risks involved. What if the Overture never becomes commercially viable? What if the costs skyrocket or regulatory constraints become a hurdle?

However, the potential upside is tremendous. The airline industry hasn't seen any groundbreaking improvements in years; the most notable changes have been limited to in-flight entertainment and fuel efficiency. With this partnership, United might change the rules of the game, secure a first-mover advantage in the realm of supersonic travel, and attract premium customers.

It's a high-risk move, but one that could pay off spectacularly, positioning United as the trailblazer in a new era of aviation.

The results of this partnership are yet to be determined. Regardless, we can share the mixed emotions of excitement and trepidation that corporate leaders such as Scott Kirby feel when they decide to take a significant risk for a potentially big reward.

DANCING TO A DIFFERENT TUNE: INFLECTION DIRECTION FOR CORPORATIONS

In the same way that inflection theory enables founders to think and act differently to create breakthroughs, it can be used by corporations to identify breakthrough opportunities and act in ways that overcome the biases of success. Companies can link inflections to fresh insights, and they also have the unique opportunity to tie inflections to their existing, inherent strengths.

Start-ups start with nothing. Their success comes from seeing what others don't see and acting in ways bigger companies would normally avoid. Without new ideas and actions, start-ups can't make a difference. Larger firms, with their established strengths, have more ways to turn inflections in their favor. Like start-ups, established companies can combine inflections with unique insights about the future, as Apple did with the iPod. Apple capitalized on newly introduced smaller disk drives to create a pocket-sized device that could hold a thousand songs, marrying technological advancement with foresight about consumer desires.

Unlike start-ups, corporations can also pair inflections with their existing strengths. When Facebook acquired Instagram, it recognized that advancements in smartphone cameras and increased mobile bandwidth were inflections that made the tiny start-up Instagram a potentially formidable competitor. Instead of reacting defensively to Instagram, Facebook saw an opportunity to play offense through what some considered an expensive acquisition ($1 billion). Facebook combined Instagram's product features with its own global reach and expertise in growth to propel Instagram to billions of users.

Inflections and insights are essential for any potential breakthrough initiative, whether for a start-up or a Fortune 500 company. These factors hold the power to amplify the potential for substantial rewards. They subject new initiatives to rigorous stress tests and are a crucial element in choosing which endeavors to pursue. Stress-testing for the underlying inflections and insights that underpin prospective breakthroughs provides a robust framework for evaluating the viability of unknown businesses—a vital exercise akin to the rigorous business planning required for established ventures. In this way, executives ensure that the same level of thoroughness and scrutiny is applied to both known and uncharted territories, fostering an environment where potential breakthroughs can thrive.

We've emphasized that, in business, the goal is never to engage in a fair fight but to establish an unfair advantage over competitors. This can be achieved by leveraging inflections and combining them with unique, preexisting assets. Apple exemplifies this strategy. When launching the iPhone, Apple didn't just capitalize on the technological inflections that made smartphones feasible; it also leveraged its unique assets like OS X (Apple's operating system), iTunes, and existing relationships with the entertainment industry. This approach was replicated in the launches of the iPad, Apple Watch, and the Vision Pro headset. The Vision Pro, for instance, utilizes advancements in motion- and eye-tracking while also tapping into Apple's established software capabilities and Hollywood partnerships. By blending new opportunities with existing proprietary assets, Apple demonstrates that large companies can indeed have an "unfair" advantage in innovation, particularly when they strategically identify opportunities that are uniquely aligned with their existing strengths.

Facebook combined the power of new inflections in mobile technology with its existing distribution and social graph when it bought Instagram. Google combined its reach with the inflection of user-generated content when it acquired YouTube.

REWARDING SUCCESSFUL FAILURE

People in big companies have careers to protect. Left to their own devices, they will pursue less risky paths and initiatives. To achieve pattern-breaking results, the CEO of a company must be committed to taking the risks necessary to win in new lines of business. Was partnering with Boom a safe bet for United Airlines CEO Scott Kirby? Heck no. But that doesn't mean it wasn't a genius move in an industry characterized by stagnation and incremental change. Right before Facebook's IPO, was paying $1 billion for Instagram, which had fewer than twenty employees and no revenue, a "safe" move? Not according to the press at the time, although hindsight remembers the circumstances differently a decade later.

Jeff Bezos, cofounder and former CEO of Amazon, actively promotes the idea of "successful failure," which turns the traditional concept of failure on its head. At the 2014 Business Insider IGNI-TION conference, he said, "I've made billions of dollars from failures at Amazon. Literally billions of dollars from failures."

Bezos believes that taking calculated risks and experiencing failures are crucial for innovation and growth. In Amazon's history, various failures have led to immense successes. The failure of Amazon Auctions, for example, led to the development of zShops, which ultimately evolved into the lucrative Amazon Marketplace. Similarly, the commercial flop of the Fire Phone served as a learning experience that contributed to the creation of the successful Echo and Alexa products. Many executives struggle to adopt this mindset, and those who do focus on learning from their mistakes as valuable lessons for future projects. Teams can fail in two main ways: either through poor execution or by taking a calculated risk that doesn't pay off. The latter type of failure isn't necessarily a bad thing. Rather than penalizing failure, some companies go so far as to offer "best failure" awards to encourage a culture of intelligent risk-taking.

CORPORATE PATTERN-BREAKING TAKEAWAYS

1. Excellence in your core business creates biases against achieving breakthroughs. The challenge for successful companies is that they often become too reliant on the strategies that made them successful in the first place. While these tried-and-true methods contribute to ongoing success, they can also become deeply embedded in the company's culture, strategy, and operations. This

makes it difficult for the company to break away from the established patterns to explore new avenues for innovation and breakthroughs. The very strengths that fuel a company's success can also make it less adaptable to change and new opportunities.

2. Avoiding failure will not lead to breakthrough success. Building the iPhone was not a safe move for Apple. It required them to negotiate an entirely new business model with the phone carriers. Facebook's acquisition of Instagram for $1 billion when Instagram had no revenue wasn't playing it safe. Neither is United's partnership with Boom Supersonic. But pattern-breaking opportunities require the leader of the company to take calculated risks rather than playing it safe and avoiding failure.

3. Inflection theory can be leveraged by corporations, not just start-ups. Inflections give corporations two forms of power to create breakthroughs. The first (same as for start-ups) is the opportunity to marry inflections with a non-consensus insight about the future. Corporations also have the added opportunity to marry new inflections with existing proprietary capabilities to enable pattern-breaking new lines of business. They can use inflections not just as a catalyst for internal innovation in creating groundbreaking products, but also as a strategic lens through which to view the possibility of creating a breakthrough through a merger, acquisition, or partnership.

CONCLUSION

No Limits

It's good to be a seeker. But sooner or later you have to be
a finder, and then it is good to give what you have found,
a gift into the world for whoever will accept it.
—RICHARD BACH, *JONATHAN LIVINGSTON SEAGULL*

When I was in the second grade, I noticed a thin book on my dad's office table. On the cover was a stylized drawing of a seagull. With its title, *Jonathan Livingston Seagull*, something about it mesmerized me.

"Dad, what's that book about?" I asked.

"Why don't you read it and tell me what you think it's about?"

That answer was pretty typical of my dad. So I decided to give it a read.

The book tells the story of a seagull who wants to fly faster than any other gull ever believed was possible. He pursues his passion, even though the rest of the flock ridicules and ostracizes him for it. (Spoiler alert: He does it! And so much more.) When I summarized it to my dad, I don't remember the exact words I used. But the idea I'd taken from it was that the biggest limits in the world are the limits of your mind, your imagination, and your actions—not the limits of the world itself.

"Not bad," he said.

Jonathan Livingston Seagull influenced my worldview more than any other book I read growing up. The other gulls saw a world of limits. Jonathan Livingston Seagull saw a world with none. The other gulls stuck with the flock. JLS was not afraid to be different. He listened to his inner voice—no matter what the flock had to say about it. He was able to break through barriers and do things his fellow gulls "knew" to be impossible. None of the other gulls ever realized their potential to break the chains of their self-imposed limits. What a tragedy for them!

If you take away one thing from this book, I hope you realize that, in different ways, all of us unwittingly let our own self-imposed limits govern how we think and act throughout our lives. The trickiest part is that they can be so embedded in our assumptions we fail to even realize they exist, not to mention how they hold us back. The same limits are true when it comes to how we think about start-ups. And by recognizing those limits, you can free yourself from them, which makes it far more likely you will become a pattern breaker and create a breakthrough that honors the gift of your time.

With start-ups, the first types of self-imposed limits come from how we think. As children, we instinctively learn unexpected new things by playing, without necessarily looking for a goal or the right answer. We create imaginary experiences of the future when we make believe that a cardboard box is a rocket ship. We make discoveries that shape our understanding by trial and error, through serendipity. We don't worry about being "wrong" when we try things. We just experience the newness and embrace what we encounter.

But as we grow up, life starts to teach us to think in ways that will limit our ability to conceive of breakthroughs. We observe that rewards come from learning how to answer questions that have already been answered. Having the "right answers" leads to good grades, a prestigious degree, or a job that pays well. In business, we are encouraged to define our objectives at the start of a project and then stay narrowly focused to meet them. We also learn to define objectives in our personal lives, like how much exercise we get or how much we should save for retirement. All these ways of thinking help us succeed but rarely lead to pattern-breaking discoveries.

In my specialty of start-ups, I've noticed that many people miss how this mindset limits finding breakthroughs. First, we often fall into conventional thinking when coming up with start-up ideas. We study large markets for gaps or ask customers about needs not met, aiming to create solutions with concrete benefits and clear market demand. But thinking in this conventional way limits us because it usually has an embedded but limiting assumption: that the future will be a new and improved continuation of the present, defined by rules already set by others. Another limit is that many others will take this common path to come up with ideas, raising the odds of fierce competition. Conventional thinking ultimately leads only to conventional success, even with smart planning and execution.

Breakthroughs are undiscovered, which means you have to answer a question that hasn't been answered yet. Only by thinking unconventionally do you have the chance to achieve unconventional success. This starts with asking better questions, such as: Are we, the founders, living in the future? Are we exploring powerful inflections? Can we develop an insight into the future that harnesses these inflections in a nonobvious way? Are we at the frontier of powerful technology, seeing firsthand how it can change our lives and the lives of others? Are we tinkering with what could signal a radically different future rather than a continuation of the present? Strong insights answer these questions and spawn pattern-breaking products, allowing your start-up to alter the game and undermine efforts by big companies that might try to fight you.

The second way we limit ourselves is through the way we act. To make a breakthrough real, you can't just think unconventionally; you must act unconventionally as well. Creating a breakthrough start-up is a provocative act. It challenges the status quo. It requires you to move people from the present that they know and understand to a different, unknown future, which means you must convince them to want to move on a different path. Not surprisingly, as you seek to do this, you will get pushback from lots of people, since most people are conventional. As it was for Jonathan Livingston Seagull, the pushback can be well-meaning (such as the resistance JLS got from his parents and friends), or it may come from those who feel more comfortable with the status quo. Some will outright dislike your attempts to create radical change, express disapproval, and hope you fail. Unfortunately, many of us are motivated by fitting in and a sense of belonging. Just as society conditions us to think in conventional ways as we grow up, it also conditions us to act in conventional ways so that we can feel a sense of belonging. Most of us would rather fit in than feel like misfits. But to move the right people to a meaningfully different future, you will need to have the courage to be disliked because the movement must be provocative enough to diverge from the status quo. The movement must break away from the flock.

Many of us seek status and belonging without even seeing it; we find it hard not to react to what others are saying, especially those whom we have been programmed to want to impress. We're reactive without realizing it. We put limits on ourselves because we buy into other people's rules. This is the fundamental limit I've observed in most people, including most founders: they define success according to rules that others have defined. But breakthrough founders have the courage to reject the need to enhance their status or approval if it conflicts in any way with the insight they have discovered about the future.

Steve Jobs, in an interview with the Santa Clara Valley Historical Association, perfectly described the way people with limiting beliefs think and act:

When you grow up you tend to get told the world is the way it is and your life is just to live your life inside the world. Try not to bash into the walls too much. Try to have a nice family life, have fun, save a little money.

That's a very limited life. Life can be much broader once you discover one simple fact, and that is—everything around you that you call life, was made up by people who

were no smarter than you. And you can change it, you
can influence it, you can build your own things that other
people can use. Once you learn that, you'll never be the
same again.

Here's how John Zimmer put it in describing Lyft: "We kept going because we really believed in our mission. I don't know if we would have thrown in the towel unless they were to lock us up."

They were willing to launch the Lyft service despite the risk that it could be declared illegal. They pushed a gray area of the law and started Lyft with a donations model in the hopes they could charge for rides before they went bankrupt. Only the success of the ridesharing movement could change the business norm of limiting the number of taxis by requiring medallions. Logan and John had to avoid charging for rides until they could work with the local government to get the laws changed. For a time, they got cease-and-desist letters every day. But they didn't get locked up. Thankfully, they didn't cease or desist.

Brian Chesky and his co-conspirators scraped Craigslist against its terms of service in the early days because they needed to find people who were already willing to rent extra rooms or their second homes. If you think Craigslist didn't love this idea and made their dislike of it clear, you would be right.

Elon Musk achieved the impossible twice, with Tesla and SpaceX, because he dared to defy the world's definitions of what was possible—and permissible. Justin Kan, Emmett Shear, Kyle Vogt, and Michael Seibel had the wrong idea at first but the right insight, which they combined with a kick-ass mentality and unconventional tactics to create Twitch and an entirely new global community centered around livestreamed gaming.

All these people had the courage to be disliked. As a breakthrough founder, you must choose to prioritize your mission for the long term, even if it means that people in the present will attack your status or sense of belonging in the short term. It takes courage to be the type of founder who is brave enough to think, feel, and act differently. Lots of people in the business world are persistent, but very few share the radical determination I have observed in the start-up founders who ultimately break through.

FLIGHT TO THE FUTURE

Like Jonathan Livingston Seagull's quest for perfect flight, our journey has just begun. Writing *Pattern Breakers* has been a fun adventure, punctuated by moments of enlightenment and occasional fits of frustration. Peter and I see this as the start of a conversation on how to achieve the extraordinary.

Pattern Breakers should be judged by its usefulness for readers. Let us know about your experience as you apply these concepts.

The future does not happen to us. It happens because of us.

ACKNOWLEDGMENTS

Books aren't written alone. This one certainly wasn't. Thanks to all who helped in this journey.

First, to our families, thank you! Your steady support and love have always anchored us while encouraging us to dream big. Mike would like to thank his "old man," Mike Maples Sr., the first to help him see that our only real limits are the ones we set for ourselves. He owes his mother, Carolyn, equal thanks, for believing in him. Mike would also like to thank his wife, Julie, and their fine bunch of grown-up kids, Sydney, Sloane, Spencer, Alexander, and Ajax.

Peter offers special thanks to his wife, Cindy, and their three adult sons, Bryan, Tyler, and Scott, and their spouses, Hillary, Tierney, and Becky.

Thanks to Mark Travis, our writing guide. He diligently turned our words into a single voice. We are also grateful to Ellen Fishbein and Bill Jaworski, who sharpened our precision with their ability to strip away the nonessential and get to our real meaning. Many hours, many drafts, even more debate: all were crucial to making this book a reality.

Special thanks to our agent, Jim Levine. Jim is a true believer in what we had to say, and he persuaded others to believe as well. Thanks to our publisher, PublicAffairs at Hachette Book Group, and our editor, John Mahaney. John, your honest edits made this a far better book. Our gratitude as well to the designers, production editors, and marketers for their fine work.

Mike would like to express his appreciation for those who provided mentorship, help, and advice along with the right balance of tough yet unconditional love: Jim Breyer, Kevin Compton, Ron Conway, Bruce Dunlevie, Kathryn Gould, Doug Leone, Christopher Lochhead, Dave Marquardt, Roger McNamee, Ginny Pangallo, Andy Rachleff, John Thornton, Don Valentine, and Bill Wood. Special thanks to the first believers in Floodgate, Judith Elsea, Phil Horsley, and Dave Swensen.

Mike wishes to thank his Floodgate co-conspirators for their support. A special nod to Lisa Del Ben, Iris Choi, Arjun Chopra, Patricia Ericson, Todd Farrell, Jay Kennedy, Mitchell Kogan, Tommy Leep, Carly Malatskey, Brooke Martin, Ann Miura-Ko, Avi Muller, Leeor Mushin, Phil Opamuratawongse, Ryland Pampush, Lori Simotas, Anne Lee Skates, Julia Wang, Tyler Whittle, Shawn Xu, and Isabelle Zhou. Their fellowship made the hard days easier. You've been helpful sounding boards and cheerleaders, and you kept me out of the wrong types of trouble!

Peter wishes to thank his colleagues and students at Stanford's Graduate School of Business. Stanford is a place that encourages new ideas and the ability to stress-test them. We see this book as a step to accelerate and elevate the discussion of where big ideas begin.

Thank you to the professors, founders, and prospective entrepreneurs who took the time to comment on our various revisions along the way. We are indebted to the help of Bill Barnett, Dennis Boyle, Peggy Burke, Glenn Kramon, Claudia Fan Munce, Joel Peterson, Andrew Powell, Tina Selig, Adam Tachner, and Bryan Ziebelman.

Most importantly, we thank the pattern-breaking founders who have changed or soon will change the future. While this book features many of their stories, the bigger message is clear: their bold ideas move the world forward, thankfully before most of us are ready.

INDEX

0

Mike Maples Jr. is an entrepreneur, venture capitalist, podcaster, and the cofounder of Floodgate, a leading seed-stage fund in Silicon Valley that invested in companies like X/Twitter, Twitch, Okta, and Applied Intuition at the very beginning of their start-up journeys. An eight-time member of the Forbes Midas List of top venture capital investors, he was one of the pioneers of the seed-investing movement, which started in the mid-2000s and now is a mainstream part of start-up funding. Entrepreneurs consider Mike more of a co-conspirator than an investor because he likes to be the first to believe in the radically different futures they pursue. He is the host of the top-rated podcast *Pattern Breakers*.

Mike received his MBA from Harvard Business School. He received his BS in engineering from Stanford University.

Outside of start-ups, Mike is a professional calligrapher and works with causes like Operation HOPE, a nonprofit organization focused on providing financial literacy and opportunity for all.

Peter Ziebelman splits his time between academia and the business world. He teaches entrepreneurs as a lecturer at the Stanford University Graduate School of Business, where he is the principal instructor for a popular course on entrepreneurship and venture capital. He has also lectured for the Wharton School and the University of Chicago. Peter began his career as part of the innovative start-up team for Speech Synthesis Semiconductors at Texas Instruments. Later he was a systems software entrepreneur at a venture-backed start-up.

In 1996 Peter cofounded Palo Alto Venture Partners, an early-stage venture capital firm that has backed several companies that were innovators in the internet ecosystem. Peter continues to consult with Fortune 500 companies on entrepreneurship, and he advises start-up companies as an independent board member.

Peter received his master's degree in management from Stanford Graduate School of Business as a Sloan Fellow. He received his BS in combined sciences from Yale University.

Peter has served on the boards of several nonprofits, including the Ronald McDonald House at Stanford, the Pacific Skyline Council, and the Stanford GSB Sloan Advisory Board. He is currently secretary and board member for the nonprofit National Council on Aging.

PublicAffairs is a publishing house founded in 1997. It is a tribute to the standards, values, and flair of three persons who have served as mentors to countless reporters, writers, editors, and book people of all kinds, including me.

I. F. STONE, proprietor of *I. F. Stone's Weekly*, combined a commitment to the First Amendment with entrepreneurial zeal and reporting skill and became one of the great independent journalists in American history. At the age of eighty, Izzy published *The Trial of Socrates*, which was a national bestseller. He wrote the book after he taught himself ancient Greek.

BENJAMIN C. BRADLEE was for nearly thirty years the charismatic editorial leader of *The Washington Post*. It was Ben who gave the *Post* the range and courage to pursue such historic issues as Watergate. He supported his reporters with a tenacity that made them fearless and it is no accident that so many became authors of influential, best-selling books.

ROBERT L. BERNSTEIN, the chief executive of Random House for more than a quarter century, guided one of the nation's premier publishing houses. Bob was personally responsible for many books of political dissent and argument that challenged tyranny around the globe. He is also the founder and longtime chair of Human Rights Watch, one of the most respected human rights organizations in the world.

•   •   •

For fifty years, the banner of Public Affairs Press was carried by its owner Morris B. Schnapper, who published Gandhi, Nasser, Toynbee, Truman, and about 1,500 other authors. In 1983, Schnapper was described by *The Washington Post* as "a redoubtable gadfly." His legacy will endure in the books to come.

Peter Osnos, *Founder*